Praise

"As a yogi aficionado, I was fascinated by Lang's tale as she gives, takes, questions, and answers through poses, shining her light and love on those relationships closest to us, and most importantly the one we create with ourselves."

LISA BARR, NEW YORK TIMES BESTSELLING AUTHOR
OF *WOMAN ON FIRE*

"Lyrical. Poignant. Funny... Jennifer's creatively structured narrative captures the essence of living as a perpetual outsider in Israel, exploring the intricate balance between personal beliefs and family expectations. A must-read for anyone seeking a profound understanding of the human spirit in a world of turmoil."

SARAH TUTTLE-SINGER, AUTHOR OF *JERUSALEM- DRAWN AND QUARTERED: ONE WOMAN'S YEAR IN THE HEART OF THE CHRISTIAN- MUSLIM- ARMENIAN- AND JEWISH QUARTERS OF OLD JERUSALEM*

"Buffeted and uncertain in her identity as wife, mother, and Jew, Lang's deeply felt yoga practice keeps her both rooted and challenged as she finds her way through the confusion of commitment to herself and others in this imaginative and inspiring memoir."

ELISA BERNICK, AUTHOR OF *DEPARTURE STORIES:BETTY CROCK ER MADE MATZOH BALLS (AND OTHER LIES)*

"Real, heartfelt, and captivating. In *Landed*, Jennifer Lang shares her seven-year journey to understand the meanings of marriage, parenthood, religion, and her connection to Israel. She discovers yoga practices and principles, and despite internal struggles and Middle East conflict, she reconnects to self and finds purpose and belonging."
TERRI L. ORBUCH, PH.D., AUTHOR OF *5 SIMPLE STEPS TO TAKE YOUR MARRIAGE FROM GOOD TO GREAT*

"In crisp, witty, heartfelt chapters—some contained in a single page—Lang chronicles her struggles to balance marriage, motherhood, Judaism, yoga, and multiple moves between the US and Israel as she bravely makes her way toward a state of mind called home."
DAWN RAFFEL, AUTHOR OF *BOUNDLESS AS THE SKY*

"In *Landed*, Jennifer Lang reminds us the root of the word 'yoga' is a Sanskrit word meaning 'to yoke'—yoking both body, mind, and spirit together, and the individual spirit with the collective one. Lang powerfully explores her difficulty yoking herself to a volatile region, using complex forms on the page to explore her complex relationship with not only the land, but also her husband."
GAYLE BRANDEIS, AUTHOR OF *DRAWING BREATH:ESSAYS ON WRITING, THE BODY, AND LOSS*

"Considering yoga is also a huge part of my life and, like Jennifer, I've spent many years living as a foreigner in Israel with my family, I could relate to what is wonderfully described in this book. Her story brought me back to a very special time and place."
EDDY TOYONAGA, CERTIFIED YOGA INSTRUCTOR AND WELLNESS INFLUENCER

About the Author

Born in the San Francisco Bay Area, Jennifer Lang lives in Tel Aviv. Since obtaining an MFA in Writing from Vermont College of Fine Arts in 2016, she's been widely published and won or been nominated for prizes for "Things Lost, Things Found" in *Under the Sun*, "Fifty Days of Summer, 2014" in *Ascent*, "The Fabric of Peace" in *Crab Orchard Review*, "Seven Definitions of Secret [See-krit]" by *Negative Capabilities Press*, "Uprooted" in *Baltimore Review*, and "Repeat the Enchanting" in *Midway Journal*.

In 2015, Jennifer created Israel Writers Studio, where she teaches ongoing classes and hosts guest teachers. For the past few years, she served as an Assistant Editor for *Brevity Journal*. When not at her desk, she is likely lifting weights at the gym or twisting on her yoga mat. Her all-time happy places are standing on her hands and teaching YogaProse: using your practice to write your story.

israelwriterstudio.com

LANDED

A yogi's memoir
in pieces & poses

Jennifer Lang

www.vineleavespress.com

Landed: A yogi's memoir in pieces & poses
Copyright © 2024 Jennifer Lang

All rights reserved.
Print Edition
ISBN: 978-3-98832-087-2
Published by Vine Leaves Press 2024

Cover design by Jessica Bell
Interior design by Amie McCracken

"When you lose touch with yourself,
you lose yourself in the world."
—Eckhart Tolle, *Stillness Speaks*

"My body is my temple
and asanas are my prayers."
—B.K.S. Iyengar

The Law of Return is an Israeli law, passed on July 5, 1950, which gives Jews the right to come and live in Israel and to gain Israeli citizenship, declaring "Every Jew has the right to come to this country as an oleh [immigrant]."

To my mother whose parental mottos
continue to guide me:
There's no harm in asking.
What have you got to lose?
What's the worst that could happen?

Preface
January 2024

Writing a book, finding a publisher, holding a copy, and promoting it takes years. In the case of *Landed,* I began the manuscript in 2016 and finished, after many false starts and multiple iterations, in early 2022.

A year and a half later, on October 7, 2023, my world, along with everyone else who calls this small and complex stretch of land home, was upended as war broke out in Israel. On that day, unimaginable brutality occurred, endless darkness descended. Everything that I thought was safe ended up being an illusion. Everything that is my greatest fear of the country where I live, with which I've grappled for decades, about which I write in my first book, *Places We Left Behind: a memoir-in-miniature,* came to fruition.

For many Jews and most Israelis and Palestinians, October 7 marks a before and after point. Revisiting this manuscript in early 2024, I was struck by how certain passages seemed irrelevant considering all that has and continues to transpire since then. It makes me wonder about one of my mother's maxims: "What's the worst that could happen?"

Was this it?

Although this book describes an earlier time, it still shines a light on what it is to be a human being living in a place that beholds both beauty and chaos.

Recently, during an interview, when asked about what's at the top of my bucket list, I responded: "This is not concrete and feels impossible, but I want to witness true peace in this small stretch of land during my lifetime. Peace for all people. Just a little peace."

Author's Note

No matter how long I live in Israel, I am and always will be considered a new immigrant. My accent will always betray me; my hardwired manners will forever set me apart.

"How long have you been here?" or "Why did you come?" or "Are you religious?" or "Where's home?" are constant conversation starters. I don't have simple, one-sentence answers. I am neither witty nor concise. This book is my attempt to answer, to find my way back to myself.

Like many authors, it took me numerous drafts before finding this story. But memoir writing is a sensitive business. Memory is slippery; perspective is personal. This is my version of the story based on my emotional truth. Every member of my family—husband, mother, sibling, children—will surely remember and tell it differently.

Most names stayed true, save for family members, who wished to remain nameless. Instead I call them Mari, French for husband, Son, Daughter #1, Daughter #2, and my sibling, ███. I recreated dialogue as accurately as memory allows and compressed the chakra scenes into one class without attributing them to a particular date or time for the sake of the narrative.

A structure geek, I often think of my container/structure and then of its contents/story. Sometimes it works in my favor, many times against—simply too confining. From the beginning, I envisioned writing *Landed* over a seven-year timeframe. Aside from my seven-year journey to finally make peace with where I was living, seven carries a tremendous amount of significance in both Judaism and in yoga. In the former, it appears many times in the Bible[1] and Shabbat happens on the seventh day; in the latter, it's the seven chakras or energy channels running from the base of the spine to the crown of the head.

Right to choose,
New York, 2011

"I need to talk to you," I said to my girls. We sat on Daughter #1's unmade bed. Magazine cutouts of shoes, purses, and clothes littered the floor in her 6 x 6-foot room. "Abba was supposed to join us but can't."

The kids called their father אבא in Hebrew even though he's French. I refrained from saying that Mari agreed to this discussion but pretended to forget. My teen and tween eyed me. They knew we weren't having more babies, their big brother was enlisting in the Israeli army, and we were uprooting to Israel at summer's end. Only four and two when we moved from the San Francisco Bay Area, our shared birthplace, they consider Westchester home.

"Well, we've been talking a lot about the move," I said. "And how different life will be there. Mostly, our Jewish life."

For the past 20 years, I'd yielded to Mari's desire to create a united observant Jewish front for our children. We abstained from using the car, computer, oven,

stove, light switches, television, telephone, and everything else electric and modern from Friday to Saturday
sundown. We observed the laws of the Sabbath, sent
the kids to Modern Orthodox Jewish schools, and
joined a Modern Orthodox synagogue in California,
New York, and again during our yearlong adventure in
Israel. While we were both Jewish, I identified as an
assimilated non-believer. For the past 20 years, I played
a role that made me feel out of place in my family unit,
in our family home.

"אבא and I have agreed that you're old enough to
choose how you want to spend Shabbat, for example."

Daughter #2 bounced on the bed. Newly 12, she still
had mushy cheeks and marble-round questioning eyes.

"I've been doing it אבא's way for a long time. Since
we're moving back to Raanana, I'll live less his way and
more mine. Sometimes I might go to a museum exhibit
or a yoga workshop on Saturday. Get it?"

"So, like if we want to go to a friend's house on Friday
night, you'll drive us?" the 14-year-old asked.

Barely five feet small, Daughter #1 stood with her
hands on her straight hips and acted as the mouthpiece
for her little sister.

I explained Friday night meant family dinner
together, a sacred Israeli tradition. And we would see
about Saturdays: if I wanted to go to a matinee, if they
wanted to go to the beach, and if we would or wouldn't
eat lunch together.

"What about our cousins?" Daughter #2 asked.

All 12 first cousins, six on my sibling's and six on Mari's side, lived in Israel and strictly observed the rules around our inherited religion. But they also had another dozen second cousins—fiercely Zionist (supportive of Israel), wholly secular (detached from Shabbat and kashrut[2]). It was complicated.

Daughter #1 giggled. "Wow, I thought we were going to get the Sex Talk. But instead, we got the God Talk."

I kissed them, relieved to have found the right words. Still, I was anxious about moving back to the country which oftentimes rattled my nerves and triggered crying jags, and we hadn't even left White Plains yet.

Root Chakra

"Okay guys, this is it," said the teacher, clapping his hands. Dressed in a tank top and shorts, he looked more like a pool lifeguard than a small business owner. "Let's start in Tadasana, Mountain pose."

Suddenly, the 50-odd men and women on all sides of me stood erect like a military regiment at roll call. I imitated even though the tallest part of me was my married name, Lang, which means long in German.

Before class, everyone was whispering, asking if Rod was back from retreat. Rod as in Rodney Yee, as in nationally famous yoga instructor, as in the man who guided my body upside down and filled my mind with sagacious words; retreat as in rubbed-me-wrong and sounded cultic.

"Okay, so we're going to work our way up the chakra system today. There are seven. Ready?"

More whispering. Some fidgeting. Since my initial class at Piedmont Yoga Studio a few years ago, I'd come every Wednesday morning barring sick kids or Jewish holidays. But I wouldn't be able to name any poses or chakras.

"Stand with your feet inner hip-width apart and press them into the floor beneath you. At the same time, reach up through the crown of your head," he said as if it were simple. "Ask yourselves: do I feel grounded, bolstered?"

The idea of rooting made me tremble. I gazed at my extremities and tried to spread my toes, imagining myself a mile up the road in my childhood bedroom. As this strapping instructor swaggered around the studio, his long ponytail swung side to side like a pendulum.

"Cool! You guys look really rooted. This is good for opening your first chakra at the base of the spine and connecting to earth energy. When your root chakra's balanced, you'll feel confident and centered, but when it's blocked or out of balance, you feel needy, insecure."

I dug my feet into the California hardwood floor, so different from the icy Israeli tiles in our apartment in Haifa, where Mari and I spent our first five years, desperate to feel the studio's warmth and weight.

Year 1: 2011-12

Balagan

Two months after the God Talk with the girls, the day after we land in Israel, we step inside the windswept-gray front door of our house in Raanana. I gasp. The late August heat suffocates me like a tight wool turtleneck.

"Alors?" Mari asks.

What do I think of a place I'd seen once, eight months earlier, in the country for my nephew's wedding, when a realtor and I stood in the foyer and my shoulders softened, saying: "You don't know our story, but I don't want to move here, yet can picture living within these walls."

She had no clue that we'd recently spent what I dubbed The Year of Living Differently in this city, to stretch our children's Weltanschauung beyond the red-white-and-blue flag. She had no idea that we'd arrived whole and left divided: Mari and Son aching to stay, Daughters and I eager to go. She had no inkling that I'd agreed to return for ten years—from the eldest entering the army to the youngest exiting the army.

Call it payback to my husband for living in my homeland for 15 years.

Call it shalom bayit[3] or peace in the house.
Call it compromise...

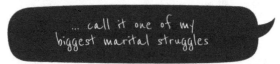

... call it one of my
biggest marital struggles

"You really want to know?" I ask Mari.

My thoughts are vicious and biting like a rattlesnake.

The girls race from room to room, shouting to each other, their voices bouncing off the stone walls, reiterating what I already know; it's a mess.

We've arrived in time for the Jewish New Year but long before the house is livable. Construction workers roam every room. Hefty tools litter the tiled floors. The kitchen countertop is MIA. New appliances stand forlorn in the barren space. Layers of grime cover every surface. Outlets malfunction. Paint splotches spot windows and walls.

He puppy-dog eyes me.

"Aze balagan[4]!"

Mari and I speak a linguistic hodgepodge—French, English, Franglais, Hebrew, Hebrish—depending on mood.

"You might want to sleep on an air mattress, but the kids and I will stay elsewhere."

I morph from upbeat into kvetch as I emigrate from New York to Israel.

Mari drops it. He neither confronts nor cajoles in his usual way. Living in America was never his fantasy, returning to Israel, never mine. My surrender came with conditions. At the top of my list: let me be.

ZIM

Days later, a mammoth truck carrying our red clay-colored container reverses into our driveway, its seven stars and three letters recognizable from afar. Six weeks earlier, it decamped from the Port of New York, heaving with our material possessions, leaving me to stare at our stripped century-old New York Tudor, the only one that ever felt like home in the 21 years of our mobile marriage, and sob.

Here, halfway around the world from my American-girl-reference point, the movers taunt us with ready-or-not-here-we-come. We're far from ready. Inside is a wreck, but outside, the sun broils me.

Mari and I watch them unload. A boy vrooms on his skateboard. A high-hanging date tree provides insufficient shade. A couple emerges from the house next door. I await the ordinary onslaught of questions: Where are you from? Do you have kids? What do you do?

After trading names and professions, the salt-and-pepper-haired veterinarian with an unmistakable Israeli accent says they raised kids on Long Island.

"I can't believe you came here when we dream of living there," he says.

I cackle to cover my desire to cry.

Mari and I exchange a long-married-couple look: save me.

A mover asks where to put our dining room chairs. Mari directs the swarm of stocky men, air-traffic-control style. I dash inside to indicate what goes where:

yoga studio

kitchen/dining/living room

bedrooms/office

Our sofa, mattresses, desks, nightstands, and flat-screen TV are encased in bubble wrap like King Tut. Cardboard boxes of books and photo albums along with Container Store bins of Legos and American Girl dolls stand tower.

As movers schlep in and out, I recall my children's favorite bedtime story, a Yiddish folk tale called *It Could Always Be Worse*. The tale of a man who lived with his mother, wife, and six children in a one-room hut. Miserable, he ran to the rabbi, who instructed him to take in the chickens then the goat, and lastly the cow until the chaos became unbearable, and his rabbi then told him to free the animals one at a time at which point the family slept peacefully and the man relished the relative quiet.

While these burly men heave and ho, I think about the civil war raging in Syria—a mere 500 miles north—realizing how fortunate we are: immigrants by choice, completely intact.

Warrior I Pose

While the girls attend school and Mari shadows the workers, I sweat on my mat at Omyoga.

The instructor, Shani, sticks closely to the 41 poses in the primary Ashtanga series, leading us from pose to pose, her words calculated and crisp, her delivery, worldly and wise. The sun penetrates through wide-open windows. No fan, no AC, pure desert heat. Her burnt umber skin glows.

I detect active verbs like lilchotz, leharim, leharchiv, making my hippocampus work intensely to recall words from Hebrew immersion class over two decades ago. My tank top clings to my torso. Buckets of perspiration drip down my sides.

Eight years earlier, during my teaching training in New York, we studied the battle between two sides of a family—the Pandavas and the Kauravas—in *The Bhagavad Gita*. Warrior I isn't about the physical warrior but the spiritual one, facing the universal enemy of self-ignorance, the ultimate source of suffering. Am I warrior enough to live here? If terrorism resurges or war ensues, am I strong enough to soldier through it? If my children grow up and leave the country, is our marriage sturdy enough to anchor me?

As I listen to 20-something-year-old Shani, everything compresses: the gray matter, the white matter, the water.

Blur

Days into our new Israeli lives, the girls and I enter the ersatz synagogue in a school gym. Hundreds of Jews sit in cheap plastic folding chairs. Day one of the two-day New Year. My eyes blur.

I don't want to be here

"Shana tova," friends and acquaintances and strangers murmur Happy New Year as we sidestep into a row.

Everyone clutches a prayer book. Married women cover their hair with a hat or scarf or cap or doily or beret or bandana. While they bow heads and sway bodies in supplication, I stare at the basketball net and stacked bleachers. Somewhere, on the other side of a low curtain[5], are Mari and Son, who stopped observing Judaism in high school but remains respectful of his father's ways. All day, we play musical chairs: stand, sit, stand, sit, stand again.

While my girls gab, I flip through the book, counting pages until the end of the service before removing my rings, passing each one from hand to hand.

Jennifer Lang

During my childhood, Rosh Hashanah only lasted one day, the siddur transliterated prayers from Hebrew, and the rabbi always told us the page number so no one could get lost. Visions of little-girl me sitting obediently in temple, pantomiming for my mother to take off her jewelry so I could fiddle and make time pass quicker. Memories of teenager-me traipsing to the ladies' room to meet my best Hebrew school friends Judy and Marcia during Rabbi Waldenberg's sermon. Recollections of juvenile-me officiating the prayer services during youth group weekend conclaves.

My ears perk when I hear "Adon Olam," the hymn sung at the end of services, a sure signpost for Jews across the globe. Outside in the yard, Mari and I chat under a tree in the abusive September sun. People wish each other a happy holiday. The kids beg to leave.

"Wasn't that lovely?" someone asks.

I refrain from answering and motion to my family: let's go!

Poser

Six days later, another holiday and countrywide closure, beginning the evening before and ending after night-fall. Erev Yom Kippur—the eve of the holiest day of the year—swells with sad air and solemn people. Complete quietude blankets a large strip of the land: no cars, no cafes, no forms of entertainment regardless of belief or observance level. Even Ben Gurion International Airport is dark. Millions of Jews abstain from food and water and stand-sit for hours in synagogue, close eyes, bang fists against chests, chant prayers, and ask forgiveness from Elohim[6] for sins they have committed over the past 364 days. On the outside, I show up for services, but inside, I bolt to a far-flung galaxy.

After synagogue, the city's main thoroughfare is awash in white—the color of purity and cleanliness—as worshippers stroll, stopping to greet friends and to wish each other an easy fast. The kids head to the house, while I accompany Mari, who wants to see and be seen.

Ahuzza Street offers an unexpected contrast. The devout repent while the secular, more than half of the city's 47,000-something residents, release. Mobs of boys race each other on bikes. Families ride with total disregard for rules of the road. Parents teach children to pedal without training wheels. Recklessness reigns. Every year, heaps of people land in the Emergency Room.

On this day, also called Festival of Bikes, I picture myself on my green Trek hybrid, cruising through the city, the cool evening wind fluttering on my arms and legs. I picture myself alone, Mari and the kids walking to and from synagogue, famished and parched. I picture myself flying and free.

Bureaucratzia

One September afternoon, Mari and I pass through
security, enter a barebones office, and sit in standard
plastic chairs. The room is vacant save for two civil
servants; one ignores us, the other eyes us.

"Closed," she says.

Mari protests like an Israeli. He explains we have a
last-minute appointment at You-Name-It Ministry and
must bring a Who-Knows-What form with our entries
into/exits from Israel for the past ten years; never mind
that we've lived out of the country almost twice as long.

"Closed," she repeats.

We need new everything:
- identity cards
- proof of residency cards
- health care cards
- city resident cards
- drivers' licenses
- municipal parking stickers
- bus passes

Our to-do list runs long like the Jordan River.

Mornings at the Ministry of the Interior, afternoons at the Ministry of Immigrant Absorption, and hours at the Ministry of Transportation. I steel myself for the chaos and inefficiency of the 1990s, when I lived here the first time, before the number system and online appointments.

"Bevakasha," he pleads as if saying please means something to her.

Mrs. Civil Servant pushes papers on her desk, bureaucracy at its best.

I stare at a poster of Shimon Peres, one-time president and two-time prime minister who, together with Israeli PM Yitzhak Rabin and Palestine Liberation Organization leader Yasser Arafat, won the Nobel Peace Prize for the Oslo Accords in 1994.

Mrs. Civil Servant asks for our ID numbers. Like actors in an American Express ad, we each recite our nine digits by heart. Time slackens. I pretend to read. Her printer sputters. More minutes pass. She summons us to her cubicle. Mari and I approach her desk.

This middle-aged woman with wiry, highlighted hair, a white t-shirt with Bonjour in silver sparkles across her chest, and a guarded smile hands us gobs of papers.

"Can I give you a hug?" I ask and open my arms.

Gratitude catches me off-guard as she slow dances into my embrace.

Sugarcane Pose

In hesitant Hebrew, I demonstrate Ardha Chandra Chapasana. With one leg on the ground and the other in the air, I strive to incorporate some relevant yogic philosophy, inherent goodness mumbo-jumbo, to remind the handful of students of the meaning of Anusara, but most concepts don't translate in this language.

When an Israeli yoga instructor called about subbing, I stumbled over his racecar-fast elocution about his small studio nestled on a moshav[7], a 20-minute traffic-clogged ride from Raanana. I didn't care about the commute and accepted, my legs spinning in hula-hoop circles.

"I've never done this before," a fair-skinned woman says in British English.

I help her, the lone Anglo among Israelis, make the hand-foot connection. She leans back. Her chest opens. "Ahhh."

"Stay in the pose and listen," I address the two dozen men and women. "Try to lift your bottom hand. As you

Jennifer Lang

balance, think about Patanjali[8], the father of yoga, and his words chitta vritti nirodhah. Chitta is consciousness, vritti is fluctuations, and nirodah is quieting. Can you find that inside?"

The one-room shack throbs with energy.

Four years earlier, in 2007, when we'd spent 12 months in the center of the country, no one in the Israeli yoga scene had heard of what was considered the fastest-growing style in America. Anusara[9] was everything I'd learned about precision and alignment on steroids. If ever I'd come close to drinking the Kool-Aid, it was Anusara flavored. For the past six years, I wallowed at Sage studio in Westchester, where my teacher edified us in the Tantric philosophy of intrinsic goodness. Week after week, I sat across from her at a teachers' practice, as well as attended workshops, taught classes, and found community.

When I asked the moshavnik about Anusara in Israel, he assured me it was coming full tilt, which made me think about the passage of time and the power of change.

"Okay, zeho. Second side, y'all!"

"When are you coming back?" the Brit asks.

Front-page news

On Tuesday, October 18, 2011, I linger in the appliance section of Mega supermarket. Flat-screen televisions affixed to the wall blare the same scoop on every channel from Yes to HOT to BBC. All week, I've been seeing the headlines:

- NPR: Israel-Palestinian Prisoner Swap Stirs Strong Debate
- *TIME*: Gilad Shalit and the End of the Israeli-Palestinian Peace Process
- CNN: Why Israelis believe one soldier is worth 1,000 Palestinian prisoners

I lean on my lopsided cart and watch the second-by-second reports of Israeli soldier Gilad Shalit, held in captivity for five years, traded for 1,027 imprisoned Arab and Palestinian suspected terrorists. First prisoner of war to return alive in 26 years. An Egyptian journalist interviews him in Cairo. Gilad is gaunt and ghostly.

"Now that you've been a prisoner, would you return to help free the 4,000 Palestinians in Israeli jails?" the journalist asks.

We gasp a collective breath.

Strangers shout "Lo yuman!" or "Unbelievable!"

This exchange divides the country: 2/3 👍 vs. 1/3 👎

Controversial like everything else here.

Gilad composes words: he's happy as long as they don't engage in terrorism against Israel.

The greater geopolitical picture is as dark and engulfing as San Francisco fog. What if PM Netanyahu liberates someone whose sole aim is to strike back, wreak havoc, and obliterate us*? No one, certainly not I, can un-remember the rampant terrorism of years prior on buses, in restaurants, and at weddings. The gory headlines:

- *The Guardian*: Suicide bomb massacre at Israeli beach disco on Dolphinarium on June 1, 2001
- *The Guardian*: The dead and the dying at Sbarro pizzeria in Jerusalem on August 9, 2001
- CNN: Passover massacre at Israeli hotel kills 19 in Netanya on March 27, 2002
- CNN: Suicide bombings kill 23 in Tel Aviv Central Bus Station on January 5, 2003

The list goes on.

When the same interview replays on TV, I head to the checkout counter. Ready to check out.

* January 2024: A chilling foreboding.

Yihiyeh beseder

One early autumnal evening as Mari and I crawl into bed, he asks about my day.

"The good news is the girls seem okay, adjusting, making friends. But the bad news is me," I say, trying to summon my alter ego, my yoga self.

"I'm listening."

"Whenever anyone hears my accent in Hebrew, they answer in English! The garbage truck never pulls over and blocks everyone behind it! The cashiers at Mega are so inefficient! Nobody ever calls back!"

I'm on a roll: the Jennifer Rant!

"Who knows when my studio will be ready down-stairs? And when I called Ella to ask about teaching at her studio in Tel Aviv, the receptionist said achrei hachagim. I'm sick of those words—after the holidays!"

"Okay, but can't you admit how much has changed?"

Shamed, I nod, the nameless, nice, Ministry-of-who-knows-what bureaucrat with the Bonjour t-shirt still in my thoughts. It's not about the garbage collectors or storekeepers or workmen. It's me.

Israel today hardly resembles the Israel of our young adult years. Then, no one formed lines at the bank-post office-supermarket cheese counter, instead elbowing each other, yelling "I'm next"; now, we take numbers and wait or make appointments online. Then, we carried checkbooks; now, we pay through direct deposits and catchy-named apps. Then, overseas brands either didn't exist or were prohibitively expensive; now, Nike, American Eagle, and Steve Madden have invaded the market.

"Change is the only constant," my yoga instructor often said. "If you resist, you'll never grow."

"You can't change the others: spouse, children, parents, in-laws, siblings," the rabbi's wife in White Plains had said at a parenting workshop. "All you can change is your reaction."

Change starts inside me.

It is the mysterious might that propelled me back to this place.

Mari snuggles in bed. "יהיה בסדר," he says every Israeli's adage.

Maybe it'll be okay, but every day I feel more and more like a sixth grader plucking petals from the oxeye daisy, chanting "I'm okay, I'm not okay, I'm okay, I'm not okay."

Hiraeth

It's late October, the sun still holding court outside, and I miss the East Coast's changing of the leaves. At least Big Box, a giant electronics store with overpriced gadgets and unsexy gizmos, is air-conditioned. While I peruse GPSs, a heavyset salesman hovers, proffering assistance.

"I speak Hebrew but can't read or write it," I say. "I need English."

He chuckles. Not meanly but matter-of-factly. He points to an updated Garmin—black and bulky—like the one that steered me through backroads and short-cuts in Westchester for the past nine years, like the one that Mari informed me wouldn't function outside of the United States.

"You have many possibilities," Mr. Big says. "Language to read map and street signs. Language GPS speaks. Language you write."

"English only."

He scrolls and says:

- Russian
- French
- German
- Lithuanian
- Swedish
- Danish
- Spanish
- Italian
- Dutch
- Slovakian
- Finnish
- Palestinian Arabic
- Jordanian Arabic
- Egyptian Arabic
- Anglit—at last

"But, it's easier, faster, if you type in Ivrit."

Confession: I learned Hebrew backwards and forwards and inside out over two decades ago but missed the aleph-bet. The 22-letter alphabet is an abjad writing system consisting only of consonants, forcing the reader to supply the vowel.

Mr. Big presses more buttons. "Queen's English or Australian English?"

I side with the Queen.

"Good luck!" he says, handing me my gadget.

In the car, I plug in my device, set country and language, and program it to Go Home.

With the AC on full blast, I allow the shadowy female to escort me to the still-dirty, still-under-construction, still-not-homey house, overcome...

Hiraeth
/ˈhir ˌ ITH/
noun
Deep longing for something, especially one's home; a homesickness tinged with grief and sadness over the lost or departed
Welsh, of Celtic origin

Metamorphosis

One Saturday in November, the girls and I drive to Tel Aviv for a Bauhaus architecture walking tour. The city that never sleeps is only 12 miles south and otherworldly.

"Feels weird," they say as we wait at the meeting spot on Rothschild Boulevard.

The rest remains unsaid, understood: to drive in a car, to deviate from old norms, to develop new ways. Today, month three, is my first attempt to implement change.

Our tour guide introduces himself. Points out the dilapidated building across the street as classically Bauhaus with its plain white plaster, clean lines, and rounded balcony. Elucidates Tel Aviv's nickname is the White City because it boasts over 4,000 such buildings, the biggest number in the International style worldwide, most covered in graffiti and gray bat droppings. Explains they were built by German Jewish architects who emigrated to Pre-State Israel after the Nazis' rise to power and eventually deemed a UNESCO World

Cultural Heritage Site in 2003. As our guide leads us through labyrinthine, leafy streets, his tongue trips each time he says this-that-the—"th" a challenging utterance for non-Americans—and describes the city's plan to renovate every Bauhaus edifice, to preserve the history of the movement. On every block, handsome and symmetrical structures are under construction, undergoing metamorphosis.

While we walk, I think about the Zen Buddhism concept of shoshin[10] or beginner's mind: having an attitude of openness, eagerness, and lack of preconceptions when studying a subject. In yoga, we call it beginner's eyes, reminding us to look at everything as if for the first time. Our cross-cultural, multilingual life keeps me in a permanent state of shoshin.

"You will see," he says to us, "if you come back in a year or two, how much will happen," but it's as if he's addressing me.

Plans

We open the never-locked front door.

"שבת שלום" I wish Shabbat shalom to everybody—great aunt, second cousins, their kids—and place a bottle of red wine in the kitchen.

"Look who's here!" says my father's cousin, only a few years older than me, while enfolding me in his arms.

"Oy, meidala," my great aunt Bruria, the family matriarch, says, addressing me with the same endearing name in Yiddish for "girl" that Zayde[11] used to call me, always adding shayna or "pretty" first. "Where's your husband?"

"Visiting his parents. If he were here, we wouldn't be. It's Shabbat," I remind her. "He won't drive."

"I forgot."

Sometimes I wish I could forget too. I love spending Friday night with our secular family...

and breaking his rules

I wish we could do it more often.

My cousin summons us for a football-team huddle. He dons a kippa, says the prayer over the wine, hands the kiddush cup to anyone who wants a sip, and repeats with the challah. Unlike in our house, where Mari belabors each one, we finish in under 60 seconds.

"שבת שלום" they say to one another, hugging as if they haven't seen one another in months even though they were most likely together a week ago. After my great uncle's recent death, my tight-knit family grew even tighter.

Everyone piles food on their plates: zaatar chicken, rice with crispy onions, chopped salad, fresh hummus, sautéed zucchini, and onion quiche. We scatter to the table, to the sofa, inside the house, outside on the porch, completely absorbed in conversation. Bruria asks my girls about their future plans.

"I'm going to the States for college," Daughter #1 says with certitude.

I'm not surprised. Aside from spending a year here when they were ten and eight, the girls are more American than Israeli or French.

Daughter #2 shrugs. I chew. Bruria eyes me. I swallow.

Son chose the army over college in America; Daughters won't have that option. Mari and I understood the implications of our move for our girls—as citizens, they'd be obligated to serve—but we never explained it. I don't have the courage tonight.

An hour later, my 80-something-year-old great aunt excuses herself and heads to her adjoining house.

Daughter #2 yawns. Son points to his watch. The uninterrupted Hebrew electrocutes our brains.

Outside, the sky is macadam black. An overwhelming stench of chicken shit reminds me of moshav life. Stars seem reachable, tangible.

"I love their version of Shabbat," I say in the car.

"Me too," my kids echo.

All three are experimenting with this newfound permission to choose: using their phones, listening to music, and surfing online behind closed doors. While I want to believe the driving force is stage-appropriate curiosity, I must own my part. Were Mari to point a finger at me, I would refuse to cower.

Humble Warrior Pose

Late autumn, I inaugurate my basement studio and begin teaching at Ella Yoga. While the former is only mine and all English, the latter hired me under two conditions: speak Hebrew and build followers.

Every time I utter a sentence, I sound like a six-year-old breaking down syllables. As I escort my students into Warriors, I stumble over unbeknownst basics: weave (fingers together), fold (forward), and stretch (arms overhead).

In New York, we called this Humble Warrior. But humble, like hundreds of words, is not in my Hebrew lexicon. Nor is devotional warrior, bound warrior, or silver surfer—all names for the same pose. No one ever says its Sanskrit name: Badha Virabhadrasana, derived from the Hindu warrior, Virabhadra.

Two months earlier, when I emailed the real estate-mogul-turned-yogi to propose an Anusara-style class at the Tel Aviv Port studio, I only shared it with Mari. Too superstitious. If I say something out loud, it won't happen. If I say something out loud, it will happen.

Never, ever, ever say something out loud that you want or don't want to happen. Thoughts are powerful. Thoughts transcend our minds. Thoughts affect our bodies.

After the holidays, Ella invited me for an informal interview. Loud waves lashed the wooden deck. Her dyed blond-and-black streaked bob framed her face, making her hazel eyes and puffy lips pop like a seasoned model. In my most polished Hebrew, rehearsed during my car ride, I shared my ideas for a heart-opening practice. When she agreed, I was so thankful I hadn't told anyone.

On an almost daily basis, I replay my yoga instructor's words: "We'll never know what we can do if we always stay safe in the pose, if we don't occasionally fall." As difficult as it is to fall, it fills us with humility[12].

"Lift up and open to Warrior II," I say after a long hold and, for once, sure of every word.

If a picture
can make you cry

During my aunt and uncle's visit, we head to Yitzhak Rabin Center, founded on the tenth anniversary of the prime minister's assassination.

On the upper level, I press play on the audio device. Like Star Trek's Enterprise, a door opens. I step into an enormous half-moon-shaped room. Two massive videos show footage from the November 4, 1995 peace rally where Rabin was shot. I rub my eyes. Outside, the corridor curves like the Guggenheim; walls heave with history, covered with boards, dating back to Rabin's birth in 1922. Beneath me, fact-filled stepping stones that march forward in time: first ATM machine (1959), walk on the moon (1969), creation of CNN (1980), collapse of Berlin Wall (1989). Every room covers a decade, each one overshadowed by war: 1948 Arab-Israeli, 1956 Suez Crisis, 1967 Six Day, 1973 Yom Kippur, 1982 Lebanon. Rabin as soldier, leader, peace broker.

I wind my way downstairs, glance at images of him with statesmen, with family, until I come face-to-photo with the most pivotal one.

September 13, 1993: President Bill Clinton, Yasser Arafat, and Yitzhak Rabin stood on the White House lawn in Washington D.C. to shake hands.

September 13, 1993: Mari and I brought our four-day-old infant home to our Haifa apartment. We sat in the living room to witness the moment on TV. I wrapped myself in a cocoon of hope, imagining the dissolution of the army, my son never having to serve.

Looking at those world leaders 18 years later unravels me.

In 1993, I was immature, ignorant, unknowing. How we'd leave Israel for almost two decades only to return. How I'd feel chasmal pulls within whether I lived in the country or on the other side of the planet. How Son would choose to enlist in the Israel Defense Forces (IDF) to defend his birthplace.

While watching the video clip of the ceremony that September day, I recall how divided my attention was between the newborn in my lap and the history ahead of me. I close my eyes and whisper private words, a prayer of sorts, to whoever will listen—Rabin, even Arafat, both long gone—to keep my baby safe.

Bifurcated I,
California, 1995

My husband and toddler greeted me in the foyer of Beth Jacob Congregation. Since settling in Oakland four months earlier, I'd honed my ideal arrival—toward the end of services, before the kiddush klatsch—on Shabbat.

Mari asked if I'd heard the news. I stared blankly at him. Son circled our legs.

"Rabin was assassinated at a peace rally in Tel Aviv by some right-wing fanatic," he said, opening his arms to cradle me.

I envisioned people lighting candles and keeping vigils in the White City. Pictured everyone from my Hebrew school friend Judy and her Israeli husband to my brother- and sister-in-law to our friends in Haifa mourning as a community, a country, together.

Last summer, I couldn't wait to leave Israel, but now, the distance shattered me. The loss of a remarkable statesman undid me. Never had I felt so torn in two.

With Rabin gone, the never-ending cycle of madness between Israeli Jews and Palestinians would probably resume. Perhaps, if we stayed in America, I could protect my baby.

So Israeli

One neither sunny nor rainy March morning, Mari accompanies Son to Tel Hashomer base for his recruitment, in some ways, our raison d'être for returning to Israel.

For the past year and a half, our firstborn has taken total control of his army process because we lived in the US, because Mari and I had never served, because Son undertakes most new challenges with extraordinary determination and single-mindedness. Never had I been so hands-off—and excluded—in all my years of parenting.

In White Plains, when Son announced his intention to enlist—and forgo or delay college—Mari and I both supported him. Neither one of us could envisage sending him off alone to a country that pampered its soldiers. We understood his longing to serve even though he could have skipped it as an Israeli-born Jew who lived abroad.

Now, here, I stay home: too early and inconvenient. Truthfully, too unbearable to watch my eldest leave. I use the girls as my excuse.

A few hours later, Mari returns, removes his shoes, clomps upstairs to the office.

"You should have come," he says. "Everyone does. Brothers and sisters, parents, grandparents, even friends. They sit at picnic tables in the courtyard and eat breakfast. Take pictures. It's a thing. Like a party. So Israeli."

Israeli as in family-oriented. As in food-related. As in celebratory. Israeli as in send your nonchalant teenagers clad in t-shirt-jeans-flip-flops clutching their cellphones and watch them transform into rule-obeying, respectful, uniformed conscripts.

Israeli as in Mari and Son for sure, Daughter #1 one day, #2 maybe, but me: no way.

Tag

As I enter Ella Yoga studio to take a class with my teacher, Shelley, ▮ calls. We played phone tag all week. Not sure if we couldn't talk at the same time or didn't want to talk. I silence my phone.

Ninety minutes later, on my drive home, the phone rings again. I pulse with vigor, answer, and open all four car windows. A baby breeze blows off the Mediterranean.

A few weeks ago, at our most recent family get-together, the topic of food—whether our level of kashrut meets their stringent requirements—erupted like a volcano. Older sib against younger sib, spouses and kids caught in our decades-old crossfire about everything from meals to prayer time. A power struggle that never ends. A power struggle that fills me with shame. A power struggle that smothers me with guilt. Because friends suggest we order acceptable food to accommodate their needs, but I refuse to kowtow to ▮'s demands. Guilt because I am a hypocrite: judgmental and self-righteous like ▮ and family and toward them, yet open-minded and tolerant with others.

In the car, now, we rehash.

"We need a break. But let's agree that even if we aren't talking to one another, we'll always speak when it comes to Mom and Dad. If anything happens. Okay?"

But memory is a funny matter. I cannot recollect who said it.

If only the baby breeze were bigger.

Roll with the flow, Israel, 1989

I came to Israel between a job in France and graduate school in America to learn Hebrew and spend time with ▮, our extended family, and childhood friends. I came because I never felt French and wasn't ready to return to America.

Five weeks into my visit, a Parisian Jewish friend invited me to a Shabbaton for Francophones with his former college classmate; Gad worked in a lab at Weizmann Institute in Rehovot, while Mari had recently completed his chemical engineering project at Technion Institute in Haifa.

Throughout the 25-hour program, during meals and discussions, Mari and I flirted. As soon as it ended, Gad invited us to play Pictionary chez lui in Tel Aviv. Around midnight, when his long-distance girlfriend phoned, Mari opened a bedroom door and curled his pointer finger like a naughty boy. He patted the bed. I complied. Like Goldilocks, he asked if the bed was good, not too hard, not too soft.

I whispered one-word answers: yes, no, yes. Time passed. Conversation stopped. The room warmed.

"Ça va?" he asked.

I was more than okay.

We inched our bodies toward one another, closing the gap between us in the darkened space.

We talked. About our parents, who were the same ages and each active in their Jewish communities; our older and only siblings, who lived/planned to live in Israel; our August birthdays; our shared hobbies like biking, hiking, skiing, traveling, reading, music, languages, movies; and our past chapters of living and working abroad. Neither of us tolerated sleeping with a battery-run clock ticking, and we both gravitated toward the color apple green.

"I'm just here for a few months," I said.

"Oui."

We stroked one another.

"I want to return to the States."

"Oui."

His hands, thick and dexterous, made my skin sizzle.

"I spent a lot of time thinking about my future career goals."

He caressed my breastbone, shushing me, saying, "Ce n'est pas important."

What wasn't important: my plans or my temporary status, what I wanted to do or where I wanted to live?

Heat and desire consumed me. My mind and body battled with one another.

Years earlier, during a sniveling airport scene, my father had said, "Try not to think so hard. Try to roll with the flow," notions that gnawed no matter where I went.

Equation, Israel, 1989

Ever since meeting a few weeks earlier, Mari and I had been traveling back and forth on the bus between Haifa (his place) and Jerusalem (mine). During our stretched-out weekends, we played countless games of backgammon and gin rummy, probed each other's bodies, and swapped childhood tales. Still, I hesitated to over-share (too much, too early), one of my biggest relationship flaws.

"Tell me how you grew up Jewishly," he said.

"For us, Judaism wasn't about belief or god, synagogue or Shabbat," I said, caressing his pecs. "We ate cheeseburgers, pork chops, bacon, and shrimp. On Saturdays, we weeded in the garden then went to football or basketball games. It was more about doing the right thing and repairing the world than praying."

My most vivid memories included dressing up like Queen Esther and parading around temple on Purim, selling candy bars to raise money for people who lost their houses in mudslides, and protesting outside the

Soviet consulate in San Francisco to free Russian Jews. Equally intense were memories of Israel: walking on the beach with Great Baba when I was five, planting trees in the Jewish National Fund Forest during a fundraising mission when I was ten, and waking up at 4:00 a.m. to pick peanuts on Kibbutz Nir Oz with my confirmation classmates during the summer of my 16th birthday.

Mari nodded.

After working as a bilingual assistant at the European Jewish Congress in Paris for the past year and a half, I knew the Reform[13] movement played an insignificant role in French Jewry.

"Et toi. How'd you grow up?" I asked.

"Just Jewish. We never had labels or movements like you in America. We practiced traditions."

"Like what?" I gawped at his dark-brown-sugared eyes.

"Our kitchen is kosher. Two sets of dishes: one dairy, one meat. At Pessach, my parents change dishes, so nothing touches hametz."

Growing up, we lugged Pop-Tarts, Fruit Loops, and other leavened foods to the basement so my mother could pile her Manischewitz macaroons and gefilte fish in the cupboards; at school, I practiced fair trade, swapping my PB & J sandwich on matzah for American cheese with mayonnaise on Wonder Bread.

"We walked to shul every Shabbat," Mari continued as if in a trance. "We ate dinner on Friday night and lunch on Saturday together. My father said blessings over challah and wine. But after lunch, I rode bikes or played with firecrackers in the fields with friends."

In many respects, Mari and I grew up more alike than different except in my Jewish life, men and women were equals.

"And the kippa?" I asked.

"My father always keeps one in his pocket and only wears it when he goes to shul. In Israel, I carry one in my backpack. But I'm not ready to wear it all the time. People make assumptions, even judge. I don't want to be judged."

(Me neither. If he wore a kippa, everyone would assume I was observant too.)

Unlike ▓, Mari didn't wear the everyday under-garment but did wrap tefillin[14] and recited the accompanying prayer ever since his father had showed him when he became a bar mitzvah.

For the past two years, while watching ▓ negate their roots and plunge headlong into Judaism, I saw an ugly, intolerant side of our religion.

As Mari and I snuggled in bed, I fixated on the math. How despite fierce attraction and intense chemistry, a simple equation did not add up:

1 believer in god/Sabbath restrictions

+

1 non-believer in god/Sabbath restrictions

≠

us

Walls,
Israel, 1985

On the last day of a mother-daughter visit to Israel, an hour before sunset on Shabbat afternoon, we hugged ▮ goodbye and hauled our suitcases downstairs to wait for our pre-reserved taxi to take us to Ben Gurion Airport for her flight to San Francisco, mine to Charles de Gaulle for the second semester of my junior year abroad. After two weeks of falafel and hummus, I craved baguette and butter.

Bundled in winter coats, my mother and I waited. And waited. And waited.

"I can't believe this!" she said.

Either the driver had forgotten or had no intention of coming. On a noiseless, picturesque street in the German Colony, there were no taxis in sight.

We brought our bags to the bottom of ▮'s building and raced upstairs, banging on the door.

"Back so soon?" ▮ said.

"Sorry, but we need to use your phone," she said.

Head shook. "Shabbes."

"I don't care. We must get to the airport!"

"I didn't say anything about you leaving before it ended, but no phone. Sorry."

For the past year, since ██ had become more stead-fast in observance, both family and friends tried reas-suring my parents, pointing out that it was Judaism, not Hare Krishna, after all. But they had no idea how alien and alienating the rules of our own religion were. They didn't understand ██'s black-or-white, holier-than-thou approach to life.

"You can't be serious!"

"Sorry."

"Really, that's going too far!" she spoke in her favorite! tone.

I'd never chosen to be her shadow or her sidekick, but it was the only place available in the family; the lime-light was occupied long before I was born, and, from my perspective, it did not appear fun. Then again, neither did jumping off the Jewish deep end nor believing blindly in a higher power.

In ██'s door jamb, I thought about how the more they were building walls between them and the outside world, the more I intended to knock them down in Paris, saying yes to anyone, everything, everywhere, anytime. Far from the rest of my family. Far from sorry.

Sacral Chakra

No matter how many deadlines loomed, how much El Niño drenched northern California, or how much nausea plagued my pregnancies, I came to class. My freelance writing clients could wait, but my psyche could not.

Rodney waltzed around the sea of admiral blue mats. In the giant rectangular space, we squished, leaving one inch between us. Outside the glass window, green vines swathed the brown-shingled structure. Mouth-watering odors of sautéed onions from Chez Simone, a charming French café across the stairwell, wafted in the air.

"Here's the thing about the chakra system. It was part of Hindu, Buddhist, and Taoist religions and called the anatomy of the human spirit. Fascinating, right?" The yoga talk helped distract me from my pregnant, awkward body. "Here goes. The next pose is Standing Straddle or Prasarita Padottanasana. Can you say that five times fast?" He chortled. "It's awesome for opening up your second chakra called Swadhisthana, sweetness."

Sometimes I thought the words sounded more Yiddish than Sanskrit. Even after all these years, the chakra shtick entered one ear, exited the other. We stood with feet wide, hands on hips, gazed up, lifted chests, folded forward, touching fingertips to the floor. My legs quaked.

"Breathe, you guys, breathe. Ask yourselves, do I feel stable?" Rodney placed his hands on the back of my head, then my neck. "Let go."

My monkey mind stopped swinging. Is that letting go?

He yammered about how you felt radiant and uninhibited, free and happy when your second chakra was in balance. "But if it's unbalanced, you might feel a lack of motivation, lack of sexual appetite, and act overly dramatic." Everything shook. "Stay with your breath." My inner thighs pulled. "Pay attention to your body."

I pictured a mythological creature straddling the globe, one foot in Israel and the other in America, my sacral center caught in a vigorous game of tug-of-war.

"Notice what you feel."

Exhausted. Energized. Everything.

Year 2: 2012-13

Forge

The month-long holidays drown us tsunami-style. I averted Rosh Hashanah and apprehended Yom Kippur.

"Last year didn't work for me," I tell Mari. "I'm not going to shul with you or walking on Ahuzza Street."

He's silent. It's dark.

"When the girls and I drove to the Conservative synagogue in Kfar Saba, an American woman invited us to break the fast with a bunch of English speakers."

Sometimes it seems like the city is 50 percent Anglos rather than the estimated 20 percent.

"Apparently, they spend the holiday at someone's house every year rather than walk two miles on empty stomachs."

After two failed attempts decades earlier, I never fast, but my kids—though no longer observant like they were raised—do, whether out of respect for their father or simply tradition. Every year, I sneak almonds or a banana or a protein bar throughout the day.

We're in bed. It's late.

"I didn't love their synagogue or the service, but the only way to figure out how Jewish I want to be is to forge new paths."

He's still silent. It's so dark I can hardly see his outline.

"I said yes."

We keep our extremities to ourselves.

"The girls agreed to come. Will you meet us?"

"Fine," he says.

"It's potluck."

I clasp his hand.

"Okay," he says, "but I'll probably be late."

"I'll make you a plate." I pulse his palm. "We'll wait for you."

Shazam

In our Israeli house, I store our passports in the room of
many names: bomb shelter, sealed room, safe room. Entering
the 10 x 12-foot windowless space doesn't bother me. Exiting
does. When I switch off the light, the brown cardboard boxes
stacked on the shelves haunt me. Five total, one for each of us:
father, mother, son, daughter, daughter. Our names hand-written in
Hebrew next to other printed big, black, bold words. More Hebrew +
English, Russian & Arabic. In uppercase, in lowercase, screaming with
exclamation points.

DO NOT OPEN!

Opening this kit may reduce its effectiveness!

Keep away from children!

**OPEN THIS KIT ONLY UNDER CLEAR INSTRUCTIONS FROM
THE REAR COMMAND!**

Storage Instructions: Keep in a cool dry place away from sunlight. Gifts
from the Israeli government: gas masks. One per citizen, including
us: new immigrants. Nonexchangeable & Inalienable. In case of war:
Iranian bomb, Hamas missiles, Hezbollah wrath. If an ear-piercing,
anxiety-inducing, rising-falling-rising-falling siren rings. If I
were writing a basal reader, it would read: *Hear siren wail. See
us run. Race to safety in 90 seconds or less. Open bulky metal door.
Turn on bright overhead light. Shut door. Run during annual
drills when army syncs cell phones with sirens. Run every
12/24/36 months because of the incessant cycle of violence
in this crazy, complex, capricious region.* On my way
out, I point at the boxes like Captain Marvel to
discharge explosive blasts of radiant energy
from my fingertips, to make the masks &
the evil that necessitate owning them
disappear.

As the door clicks shut, I shout

Shazam!

As if,
Israel, 1990

One day in early August, Mari called from work while I was getting dressed for school, asking if I'd heard the news.

If crying was my default coping mechanism, then avoidance was my default defense mechanism. When the 9:00 p.m. news began, I exited the living room. Upon hearing the three beeps signaling hourly broadcasts on the car radio, I changed stations. Reading the daily headlines in the newspaper was unmanageable: too much passive tense, too many army acronyms, too real, too close, too frightening.

"Saddam invaded Kuwait. He sent over 100,000 soldiers with hundreds of tanks early this morning, while we were sleeping. Il est fou[15]."

(Il = Saddam or Mari?)

The roam phone moans.

"Ça va?" he asked.

The stakes were evident: Iraq had accused Kuwait of flooding the world market with oil and demanded compensation for oil produced from a disputed field on their shared border. Previous attempts to resolve the dispute had failed. Iraqi PM Saddam Hussein wanted to right the perceived wrong in a region where war was often both the default coping and defense mechanism.

"Now what?" I asked as if he were a seer.

Our wedding was in five weeks. Overseas guests were due to arrive from France, Germany, and America. In this crunch time, I wanted to hog the spotlight.

"Saddam's bombing Kuwait City like crazy. He established a provisional government, threatening to destroy it and anyone who challenges the takeover by force. Ne t'inquiète pas," he said as if telling me not to worry would make my worry disappear. "It won't affect us. It doesn't involve us. יהיה בסדר!"

He tossed out that Israeli maxim like a bag of garbage, but I knew better. Nothing was going to be okay. Certainly not me.

Lire,
Israel, 1989

At the French Shabbaton, Mari and I read together.
After dinner on Friday night, we sat on the stiff, industrial sofa in the lobby.

"Tu veux lire?" he asked, showing me *Sha'ar Lematchil*
newspaper for beginners and immigrants. Since he'd
begun ulpan six months earlier, he played teacher.

I stared at the big, block letters. He explained that
in most papers, the alphabet consists of consonants,
holding the reader responsible for supplying the appropriate missing vowels, but this one included them.
I picked a headline with the only name I recognized:
Yitzhak Shamir, Israeli PM. I sounded out the letters
as Mari slid his pointer finger under each one, moving
right to left.

By the end of each sentence, I'd forgotten the beginning. Frustrated, I pushed away the paper. He continued.
When he stumbled over a new word, he glanced at
the glossary box and returned to the article to piece it
together, persistent and determined. Between us, we

understood Shamir's government had suggested an end to the violence and elections in the West Bank and Gaza.

He set down the paper. His biceps surged under his wrinkled button-down shirt. Participants lingered, talking, playing games. I had no interest in meeting any of them, only this lanky, leggy man next to me, and wondered if the magnetism was mutual.

Launch

In the Association of Americans and Canadians in Israel Tel Aviv office, I write William Zinsser's words on the whiteboard: "Writers are the custodian of memory and memories die with their owner."

After two years of teaching creative nonfiction classes in our previous New York life and after months of preparing and promoting an English-language memoir class (not a given in a Hebrew-speaking country) in Israel, I was grateful people registered. I couldn't wait to create a community, dive into the material, and listen to their stories.

Gate Pose

As the smell of sandalwood spreads around the corners of my T-shaped yoga studio, I think about other incense-infused places where I've practiced like Thailand, Berlin, and Los Angeles. Which makes me think about my potpourri of practitioners from London, Toronto, Boston, Belgium, Brazil, Johannesburg, and Jerusalem. Which makes me think about where I've come from and where I've landed. Which makes longing release at jet-plane speed.

Being here at this moment in time is tough. If I could fly away every time this country heated up, I would.

"Parighasana or Gate pose goes low. Do you feel it between your ribs, down your leg?"

I observe my students, a hodgepodge of ages and abilities. When my neighbor, a second-generation Sabra[16], arrived with her college-age daughter, I asked the occasion. Her one-word answer sufficed: המצב

AKA Hamatsav

AKA The Situation: a euphemism for political unrest, operation, war, suicide bomb spree, or general malaise du jour

AKA Now: Hamas on a missile-firing rampage from its Gazan outpost into southern Israel

A student at Ben Gurion University in Beersheva, her daughter explained campus is closed until further notice. There, civilians have 15 seconds to reach shelter; where we live, in the center, we have a luxurious 90.

"Try to tune into your breath, out of your heads," I say.

An American woman, her face creased with origami worry lines, blurts, "How? My husband was called to reserve duty at the border and went even though his back is killing him and he's old enough to be their father so I'm alone with four kids and so scared that I can't sleep."

Who am I to tell her or anyone in this room to relax? What do I know about sending my husband to battle?

Instead, I tell them to switch legs, trying to ignore my own spinning mind, consumed with I'm-definitely-not-warrior-enough-to-live-here thoughts.

Queen of
compartmentalization

"Did you hear about the sirens in Tel Aviv?" Son asks during dinner.

Six months into his army service, he sleeps at home and commutes to a nearby base.

Mari responds, his mouth full of food, saying "First time since the Gulf War, when Mommy and I lived in Haifa."

Air-raid alarms blare near Gaza, but this is different: the middle of a country 33 times smaller than Texas, 12 miles from our house.

what the f***?

"Can we change the subject?" I ask.*

"I don't get it," Daughter #1 says. "You agreed to move here, but you don't want to know what's happening? What'll you do when I enter the army? And her?" She points at Daughter #2.

At what moment in the last six months, since our Shabbat dinner with my great aunt, had she grasped that after high school comes the army, then college?

"In New York, I told אמא my decision to disconnect. I don't want to hear about Hamas, Hezbollah, Iran, Shmiran."

I keep the rest to myself:

Because Israel's physical location and geographical proximity to Syria and Lebanon, Egypt and Iraq make me puke.

Because war and I go way back.

Because this region remains trapped in its own Catch-22: neither side capable of nor willing to refrain from violence and embrace peace, forever entwined in a game of tit-for-tat.

With Son in the IDF, I tilt my head down. When the girls tell me they practiced running to bomb shelters at school and learned to log onto the Ministry of Education's website in case of school closures during war, I tune them out. As long as I divide everyone and everything into separate boxes (yet another phenomenal defense mechanism):

family + friends

missiles
+
military

dream at night

"Whatever, Mommy," Daughter #1 says.
"You do you," Daughter #2 says.
Mari and Son smirk. I clear the dishes.

* January 2024, I cringe while rereading this, realizing how childish
I sounded.

Voice,
Israel, 2008

During the second part of our Year of Living Differently, Mari and I often slept back-to-back, each swaddled in blankets of anger.

One evening, he proposed biking to Raanana Park to talk. We faced each other on a bench next to the wooden play structures.

"I wish you were willing to stay," he said. "But I get it."

My fists unballed.

"So, if we leave for New York this summer, would you consider coming back? Not this school year but the next?" he asked.

Under the obscure night sky, I remembered each one of our therapists—Haifa, California, New York—urging me to find my voice.

"I need to go home for closure. But I'm willing to consider coming back," I said cautiously.

whose voice was this?

The 2006 Second Lebanon War aside, the security situation had much improved; suicide bombings had reached a record low. And, as Mari pointed out, I enjoyed certain aspects of our Israeli life: its proximity to Europe, Africa, and Asia for travel, our children's novel independence, living history in real-time.

"But I only agree to return in three years, after the kids' milestones." Two graduations—one high school, one middle school—and one bat mitzvah.

Mari remained mute. Not responding had become his modus operandi this year during our fiery deliberations. I wanted to shake him, to make the words spill forth like the game of Boggle.

He squeezed my hand. A mosquito buzzed. Animals from the petting zoo squawked. Birds cawed. On that spring evening, we looked around us, at each other, and listened.

Suspended animation, Israel, 1989

Seated in Hebrew class—five hours a day, five days a week—in Jerusalem, I glanced at my watch, fully aware that in minutes the country would call us to attention. Even though this was my seventh trip, I'd never been here during the springtime, secular holidays.

Outside on Jaffa Street, our ulpan teacher shushed us. A formidable noise wailed. For two minutes, every passerby and vehicle stopped, stood, and bowed heads respectfully. In a country where it's often difficult to be heard above the din with impatient drivers honking, falafel vendors shouting, and delivery trucks thundering, I was stunned by the suspended animation as if someone pressed a pause button.

Growing up in northern California, I never paid attention to Memorial Day. Besides the Highland Avenue parade, we neither sang "The Star-Spangled Banner" at a school assembly nor visited a cemetery to pay tribute to fallen soldiers. Vietnam, Korea, and World War Two wars were not mentioned. Memorial Day meant a long weekend, less homework.

At a busy intersection in the heart of Israel's holiest spot, I swallowed to avert the sting of tears. Being here, witnessing this singular moment in this small place, meant something. My presence mattered.

After returning to our classroom, I closed my eyes to concentrate. To stop the clock. To disregard inquiries concerning my future. For now, I wanted to remember the ferocity of the siren, the all-encompassing stillness, the inimitable melting pot of people in this intricate slice of land. I wanted to remember how much my cousins and every soldier had done, do, and will continue to do to protect it. I wanted to remember how awe burrowed in my bones, how wonder left me wordless.

Kind of funny,
kind of sad

In the Mega checkout line, I pack the customary eggs/
cheese/cold cereal with the uncustomary wafer cookies/
Snyder's pretzels/Pringles. For the past week, emails
have arrived, beseeching us to send sealed edibles to
hungry soldiers during Operation Pillar of Defense.
Tomorrow, a convoy will transport provisions from
Raanana to some unnamed base.

After stuffing my plastic bags into the tiny trunk,
I speed down Weizman Street as if being chased. On
the radio, Tears for Fears croon "Mad World." Urgent
planes zoom overhead. As I unpack, Mari arrives and
picks up the chips.

"Don't touch! They're for the army."

"Didn't you hear? It's over."

He chuckles. A cynical, sarcastic, black-humored
chuckle.

One hundred and ninety-two hours of missile lobbing
and sirens and running for shelters for a swath of the
country.

He pries open the lid and pops a Pringle. I open my palm.

Mad indeed.

True

At my desk, I read "The Colonel" poem by Carolyn Forché, who tells us she ate a rack of lamb and drank good wine at the colonel's house with his family, while a savage civil war raged outside, and, after dinner, he dumped the contents of a grocery bag containing an assortment of human ears like dried peach halves, saying, "... tell your people they can go fuck themselves," before sweeping them to the floor with his arm and holding his wine in the air.

1979 El Salvador.

2012 Israel.

Terror never ends.

Nowhere,
New York, 2001

Seventy-nine days after settling in White Plains, Mari called from work, imploring me to sprint to our attic office and turn on Baba's castoff television set.

On every channel, grotesque images growled:

Twin Towers
stretched skyward

a plane careened into one

then the other

both buildings ablaze

stygian smoke

random bodies

leaping from ledges

still more bodies

still leaping

free-falling

too gruesome to watch

too impossible to ignore

nothing like Israel

everything like Israel

tragic and violent

grief and gut-wrenching

"See," my spouse said, "terrorism is everywhere. Nowhere is safe."

Small victories

At a local school, I flash my ID at the security guard. He points toward door number 35. I hand my teudat zehut to three retirees, explaining it's my maiden vote in Israel. One says mazel tov! Another one points at the isolated booth—a royal blue triptych—standing expectantly in the middle of the classroom.

The sole democracy in the Middle East, Israel has an unwieldy, ever-changing number of political parties: 34 this time. Meaningless words swim across the boards abbreviated in two- and three-letter acronyms. I scan right to left in search of my preferred party, the only one which aims to impose army conscription on the Ultra-Orthodox, like ■'s sons and daughters.

"We might be here all day," I joke in Hebrew. A wall clock ticks. Outside, laughing doves and hoopoes yap.

A bronze-haired woman offers to help. When I say Yesh Atid, whose corresponding letters are Yud, Ayin, she points to Pey, Hey, retrieves a flimsy white slip of paper with two black letters and the party's full name from a hook, snatches the envelope from my hands, then tells me to enclose the paper and lick the seal. How can a nation with more high-tech start-ups and a larger venture capital industry per capita than any other one in the world have such a rudimentary voting system? I slip the envelope into a blue box on a table, retrieve my ID, and exit.

Off the mat

After class, Ella summons me to her office. The sea rollicks behind her glass windows. The studio owner asks if I heard the news.

I nod. My Facebook feed was inundated by the un-ignorable headlines:

- *The Washington Post*: Scandal contorts future of John Friend, Anusara Yoga
- *The New York Times*: Yoga and Sex Scandals: No Surprise Here
- *New York Magazine*: Yogi John Friend's Karmic Crash

In response, my entire community in New York renounced their affiliation. The fastest-growing system of yoga catapulted from grace. And I, thousands of miles away, grieve alone.

"I'm sorry," Ella says. "Such a shame. But I'm mainly sorry because you don't have the minimum required students to keep your class."

"I've loved the opportunity to teach here. You've created a beautiful community," I say, rising to leave.

"Where do you practice?"

I open my palm with a voilà.

She locks eyes with me. Her hair, a different color and cut every time, is a crisp gray-blue bob. "You may come as my guest," she says, bowing.

"Toda raba."

Context

When a missed call from Son flashes on my phone, I dial immediately. (He never calls during the day.)

"Hi, Mommy," he answers on the first ring.

(I melt when he calls me Mommy.) In the background, commotion. (Especially now.) Sirens howl. (In uniform.) Total chaos. (Even though he wears civilian clothes, I've seen him in his olive green ensemble.)

"I'm in the hospital, but I'm okay. There was a car bomb in Tel Aviv. I was on a bus next to it. It was the mafia, not terrorism. Bus windows exploded. Glass flew everywhere, in my hair, on my clothes."

(When was the last time he said this much in one conversation?)

When I offer to come, he declines because he must return to the base.

"You sure you're okay?" I ask before hanging up.

He assures me with that same two-syllable, too-casual-for-the-context word.

(I follow his lead, thinking like Mari, like Son: calm, stoic, solid.)

Grip,
Israel, 1991

Deep asleep, wed only 131 days, Mari and I were roused by an ear-shrieking, skin-tingling, mind-bending air-raid siren. In silence, we sprinted to our guestroom, sealed ourselves in with duct tape, ripped open the cardboard boxes from the cupboard, tightened the black rubber straps behind our skulls, peered through two titanic holes, removed protective guards to breathe through the nose pieces, and waited.

"Ça va?" he asked, gripping my hand.

The tar-black sky thundered with incoming missiles possibly carrying lethal chemicals aimed at us.

How could I, a 25-year-old American immigrant who has never experienced anything beyond seconds-long earthquake drills and tremors, be okay?

How could he?

Uncertainty gripped me.

Would I ever be able to accept that the home we were trying to build could periodically, potentially collapse?

Nothing felt certain save for the sound of that siren.

Alterations

Friday, Daughter #1 and I enter Maya's, an odd mix of Old-World tailor—plastic grocery bags of clothes, low-tech Juki sewing machines, fabrics and ribbons and threads strewn throughout the room—and New World hang-out. Too many bodies in the cramped space: one changes clothes behind a chiffon curtain, another inspects her potato sack, inside-out army uniform in the full-length mirror like a princess before the ball. Maya, in tight jeans and tired black boots, measures every seam. Soldier Girl beams. Maya pins the outer edge of the legs, inner thighs and waist, tailoring it like a GAP skinny pant. Fascinated, Daughter #1 watches.

Dressing-room Girl places her uniform on the counter and everybody do-si-dos.

"That'll be you soon," I whisper.

My chatty child nods, a silent acknowledgment: finish high school in two years, serve in the army for two years.

At 1:00 p.m., minutes before closing time, the harried seamstress pins my daughter's little black dress for her sweet 16 tea party. She admires herself but can't take her eyes off Soldier Girl. Their eyes meet in the mirror, and I take a picture.

Handstand Pose

Shortly after befriending Shani, I proposed a weekly teachers' gathering. Ever since, we've been meeting on Tuesdays, alternating between our studios, each of us taking turns leading in Hebrew or English. This week, our leader kicks into handstand, her ponytail dangling in front of her nose.

"Listen," she says. "While you're here, think about Patanjali's call to practice. Does it matter whether we're upside down or right-side up?"

His idea was to calm the mind through the meditative techniques of yoga. Hers is to show us the calming and meditative side of inversions.

I drag my mat to the wall, stick a block between my upper thighs, and kick both legs simultaneously, lithe and airy. Each time I invert, I hear my Sage yogis urging me to use my legs more.

While squeezing the block, I survey the room of yoginis. A stunning mix of bodies and backgrounds from Russia, France, Mexico, and beyond, each of them firmly rooted to this complex place. Seconds tick.

I squeeze harder. Heat travels to my head. I squeeze again. Wondering if, one day, someday, I'll share that sensibility, understand that connection.

Sabbatical, Israel, 1992

Five years after receiving my B.S. at Northwestern University, between completing my M.A. course-work and beginning my thesis at University of Haifa, I received a letter inviting me to pursue a Doctor of Philosophy in International Relations.

When Mari asked my motivation, I said a sabbatical every seven years. The thought of spending a year in California appealed to me; the grinding research and pressure to publish did not.

Two years earlier, my hot-off-the-chuppah husband raised our complicated reality: him from one country, me from another, our parents elsewhere. That I'd married the place as much as I'd married the person was obvious. Less obvious was an exit strategy, which made me ponder a Ph.D.

When I'd suggested moving every seven years—Israel, France, America—I had no inkling how far-fetched and draining it would be mentally, physically, and emotion-ally. Clueless that rooting and uprooting would leave me feeling dépaysée, a difficult-to-describe French adjective: situated in unfamiliar surroundings, being out of one's element, displaced, astray.

Rite of passage

In the hosts' swank living room, 21 tenth graders, 42 parents, plus a gaggle of grandparents, siblings, and faculty celebrate our teenagers receiving their own ID cards. For most, it's a purely administrative process at the Ministry of Interior, but their principal infuses it with meaning. After introductions and formalities, he asks an Israeli parent to hold up his blue, worn, plastic bifold.

"Why is the teudat zehut so special?" the father speaks in slow Hebrew for the benefit of the new immigrant parents.

Another Israeli answers: "Because it lasts forever. If we grow old and look back, we'll see ourselves stuck in time as 16-year-olds."

Everyone twitters. In addition to a unique nine-digit number, first and last names, father's and mother's names, date of birth (both Gregorian and Hebrew), ethnicity (if issued before 2005), gender, place and date of issue (both Gregorian and Hebrew), and a color portrait photo, it comes with an appendix that contains current address, previous addresses, previous name(s), citizenship, name, birth date and identity number of spouse and children.

"If you ever replace this document and your kids are over 17, their information no longer appears because they're no longer your dependents." We newcomers don't discern these facts. Our cards are one, three, nine years old. "The same is true if you lose a child, in the army or an act of terror."

A weighty, collective sigh. After each student receives his/her card, the principal asks us to rise for "HaTikva." As we rise to sing the national anthem, I dab my eyes.

Dialogue

For the past eight months, Daughter #2 has spent every Friday morning with a mixed group of middle schoolers—Israeli Jews from Raanana and Arab Muslims from Tira—in a pilot program, in English, to foster dialogue and break down barriers. Today, we celebrate them. Sitting in a semi-circle in front of the audience, they hoot. Daughter waves shyly.

Two by two, the kids take turns introducing each other. The Jewish teens, most of whom come from Anglo upbringings, have an unfair linguistic advantage over the Arabs. Arabs learn Hebrew as their second language in third grade, English in fourth grade. Some, but sadly not all Israeli Jewish children, learn Arabic in junior high.

Daughter #2 makes eye contact with her partner before speaking: "This is Nadine. She moved here last year from America. She's also 13 years old and lives in Tira with her family."

Then Nadine points to Daughter #2, saying, "She moved from New York to Israel last year. Her father is French. Her mother American. She has one older brother and one older sister."

The room applauds. "Wow! They knew everything about each other!" the kids clamor.

Before leaving New York, I told my yoga students at Sage about my vision of teaching yoga to Arabs and Jews, using the practice as a language of peace and coexistence. Even if it doesn't materialize, maybe this experience will spark something in Daughter #2.

I blast with love. My Jewish daughter and her first Muslim friend smile, bow, and take seats on opposite sides of the room. Maybe one day, they'll sit together.

What would you do?

One May morning during my parents' annual visit, we tour south Tel Aviv with an American social activist, who introduces us to Adam, a 28-year-old Darfurian with marshmallow white teeth and a beanpole torso.

"I come here to share with you my journey," he says in faltering English. "Ten years ago, when I escape Sudan, I lose everything. My family. My roots. Israel let me in. Since then, I do anything for work: cook, garden, clean. Because you understand I have no papers, no status."

Oh, his story. Oh, the relentless sun. Oh, the scent of men in need of showers. Adam explains that many sleep in Levinsky Park because of overcrowded apartments. At night, they pile insubstantial mattresses beneath plastic-coated play structures under a low-hanging tarp.

All morning, as we explored the area surrounding the Central Bus Station, the guide distinguished between refugee, migrant, labor migrant, and asylum seeker, totaling approximately 60,000. She explained when, why, how they arrived, and how the country manages the influx of Other. Regardless of their roots—primarily

Sudanese and Eritrean—they face prejudice in a country created post-World War II, post-Holocaust as a homeland for the Jewish people. Nationwide controversy strikes again.

"Why do you stay?" an Israeli man asks.

Adam fixes his eyes on us: "What choice do I have?"

Full-body goosebumps sprout despite the grueling heat.

As we walk along Neve Shaanan and Levanda streets, our guide points out churches of diverse denominations, Asian-Indian-Ethiopian grocery stores, and grassroots organizations to aid these people from not-so-far-away lands. At our last stop, I whiff jasmine incense mixed with fried onions.

"Why do they stay if it's so hard?" a British woman asks.

"They can die here or die trying to go elsewhere," the guide says. "What would you do?"

On the way home, as my parents discuss how eye-opening that was, the word "choice" bounds in my brain.

Sold

All day, everywhere I go, everyone speaks in full sentences and fragments, in "oh my god!"s and "did you hear?"s and "can you believe?"s.

When I turn on the radio, announcers mention "It" after every song.

"It" is four letters, a catchy name, a spin on a homonym.

All day, everyone talks about how a no-named Israeli started a company in 2008 in the industrial zone of Raanana, one block from Mari's office and 1.6 miles from our house and sold it to Google for $1.3 billion.

At the dinner table, "It" starts over again.

In full sentences and fragments in "oh my god!"s and "did you hear?"s and "can you believe?"s.

And I, the one who didn't want to come and on difficult days still doesn't want to be here, am caught up in the excitement and caught off guard this time by a fervor to revise the bomb-shelter basal reader and shout:

"Look at us! We've got WAZE! There's more than war here!"

Sun Salutations

On the boardwalk of the Tel Aviv Port, a distinguished Ashtanga instructor invites us to stand in Mountain pose. A plethora of practitioners rise. Alongside us, passersby rove, ride Segways, scooters and bikes, push baby strollers, slurp ice cream, and tote shopping bags.

I behold Judy, who still resembles a high school gymnast despite three kids and four decades. While I gorged on buttery apple tarts during my junior year in Paris, she explored her Jewish roots at Hebrew University in Jerusalem and fell in love with a Sabra.

Here for Ella Yoga's summer solstice 108 Sun Salutations[17], we flow in a sea of yogis: nursing moms, off-duty soldiers, tattooed retirees. Photographers patter around our mats, climb atop the studio's roof, and click their cameras. The instructor finds new ways to say the same thing, mixing Sanskrit and Hebrew, counting the nine poses of each Surya Namaskar.

"Jenny, look," Judy says.

I glance west. The sun, a gigantic burst of bright orange, glows during its descent.

"I love this," I say, even though my nemesis, Mademoiselle Ambivalence, tries to insert herself with "Are you happy? Do you feel safe? Can you stay?" I focus on the flow, shoving her aside.

The teacher dedicates the last eight to Ella, to her staff, and to the workers at the port.

"For the final one," he says, "dedicate it to someone important, on your mind, in your heart."

I picture Mari.

Future,
Israel, 1989

On our third weekend together, we tossed our towels under a shaded structure at the beach in Haifa. I eyed Mari's tight-fitting, slinky suit, so unlike our oversized American ones.

Waves roughhoused. Surfers and sailboats bobbed. My body shuddered. Ever since a near-drowning incident in seventh grade, I'd avoided ocean water. Would he hold my hand and protect me? I asked. He grinned.

"But can we talk?" Sometimes we didn't do enough of that; sometimes we didn't reach the end of a conversation; sometimes we didn't resolve our differences of opinion. After a serious relationship with an American Jewish man with whom I analyzed every interaction, less talking appealed to me. "I'm only here temporarily." He eyed me. "Because I'm starting school in the States."

It had taken me two years to determine my next step: a Master's in Public Policy. I envisaged changing the American school system, introducing a second language in elementary school like English in Europe and Israel.

"My mom called to tell me I was accepted into three programs so far."

He kissed and congratulated me.

My thoughts bucked and lurched: could I forfeit my plans? Defer a year? Roll with the flow?

"Come," he said.

He called as a wave hit. Encircled my waist with his hands. Hoisted me above the gush of water. I wanted him to hold onto me and lift me over every wave.

Solar Plexus Chakra

While most classes at the studio lasted 90 minutes, Rod's took two hours.

"Ta da, we've arrived at the third chakra. Located at the navel center or solar plexus, it's the core of our identity, personality, and ego. Think about that. The core of our ego lies beneath our belly buttons."

The room tittered. Years ago, I used to glance at the clock but now, I never wanted class to end. Afterwards, I felt taller, sturdier, and focused. The constant mental chatter disappeared. Sometimes even the judgment did too.

"Okay, so Revolved Trikonasana, here we come." He laughed like a crazed scientist then directed us: right, left, up, down, extend, inhale, exhale. When Rodney reminded us to root down through our feet, I weeble-wobbled.

"Excellent. Do you feel the stretch down the backs of your legs? Along your spine? This pose opens your chest and stimulates your abdominal organs. You with me?"

I was with him. It didn't matter how many times I'd done this twister. My kishkes burned.

When balanced, Rod said, our relationships with our surroundings were serene. When imbalanced, however, we strived for control and authority, obsessed over minute details, and saw life through a pro-con lens, losing sight of the whole picture. Bottom line: me. A control freak, I flipped when the laundry basket was overflowing, the kids screeching, and the deadlines pending.

"This chakra is about power, stability, and perseverance. It's about asking yourself if you're open to all possibilities that life has to offer. Are you?" he asked.

Year 3: 2013-14

Surprise

As we plod upstairs to the women's section, I regret my decision to come. Spending 72 hours—the two-day Rosh Hashanah holiday ending as Shabbat begins—is restrictive[18] enough. When I agreed to celebrate the holiday in Jerusalem to break routine, I didn't expect to attend services.

In the U-shaped balcony, Daughters and I sit near the Torah Ark. Built in 1982, the Great Synagogue merits its name with vertical stained-glass windows, red velvet seats, and chandeliers. Its modern, clean interior is nothing like the old shtetl, hole-in-the-wall shuls around the country.

"Look, there they are," Daughter #2 points downstairs at Mari and Son, white tallits draped over their wrinkled shirts and kippa-covered heads.

Daughter #1 shushes her. They open their prayer books and search for the page. I keep mine closed on my lap.

After the major holidays ended last year, I distanced myself from the dutiful parent role. Reminded myself of my God Talk with my girls: how they'd learned the do's and don'ts and become adults in the eyes of the Jewish community at their bat mitzvahs and been deemed mature enough to decide for themselves if they wanted to observe this lifestyle.

A chorus of men's baritone notes harmonize familiar words: "Mi cha-mo-cha, Av Ha-Ra-cha-man."

A surprising rush of connection runs up and down my arms and legs. Connection to my roots: Reform movement, Camp Swig, Northern California branch of National Federation of Temple Youth, Judy and Marcia, my long-term boyfriend. Eyes closed, I listen. Not because I relate to the hymn or comprehend its words but because I feel something. Something buried inside me. Something lost, aching to be found.

Bombard,
Israel, 1989

During our first summer playing house, late one Friday afternoon, Mari and I cuddled on his bed. When he asked if I wanted to accompany him to services at a neighborhood synagogue, I declined. When he asked why, I told him the truth.

"I hate how the women's sections are either upstairs or behind a curtain. Like we're inferior or invisible."

He caressed my face. My stomach fluttered. Opposition assailed me. I wanted to be with him, yet I didn't want Judaism to dominate our dynamic, didn't know how to balance what I did and didn't want.

"What else?" he asked.

"The service is all in Hebrew, difficult to follow. Plus, the prayers and tunes are different."

He shook his head, saying "Quel dommage."

Maybe it's a pity. Maybe not.

From senior year of high school to senior year of college, I dated someone from a similar background. We shared Jewish camp friends and reference points.

Until some indistinct day during my junior year abroad, when different became more alluring than same. When my dream of being French, speaking several languages, and living overseas outweighed everything else. But in that search to share my life with someone who grew up another way, had I neglected to hold onto my own way, the essence of my identity?

Between ▮, Boyfriend, Baba and Zayde, I felt bombarded by Judaism. Being in Israel, where every aspect of life revolved around Shabbat and holidays, sufficed. Always the Good Jewish Girl, I shoved aside those thoughts, instead swimming my tongue around the insides of Mari's mouth.

Split at the root,
California, 1974

In Piedmont, a small residential city surrounded by Oakland on all sides, Jews made up less than ten percent of the population. Every year starting in kindergarten, my mother visited my classroom to read a picture book about Hanukkah, light candles on a menorah, and fry latkes on our portable electric griddle. She liked explaining how important it was to share our differences, but I hated being singled out as Other.

One December day, I arrived from school starving and shouting, "I hate being the only Jew in my class!"

Being Jewish meant I alone missed Mrs. Meaney's math test on Rosh Hashanah and Yom Kippur when we sat in temple all day. It also meant feeling excluded when our music teacher made us sing "Silent Night" and only included "I Had a Little Dreidel" at my request.

"I'm sick of being different! Please, please, please can we get a tree this year? Like everybody else," I pleaded, running up to my room, ready to slam my door. "Besides, you had one when you were my age. It's not fair!"

My mother knocked. Belly down on my trundle bed, I tugged at the green-and-yellow shag carpet.

"You're right," she said, stroking my forehead. "I grew up with a tree and think it's okay to have one. For me, it doesn't mean anything more than it's pretty. That's why I put greenery on the mantel. I'll ask Dad but no promises." I crossed my fingers, hoping this would finally be the year the Friedmans got one.

That year, ███ deigned themselves Super Jew since they were learning to read from the Torah for their upcoming Bar/Bat Mitzvah. Not only did they refuse to help in my tree crusade, but they also excused themselves when my parents beckoned me to the living room. I slumped on the sofa opposite them, avoiding all eyes.

My father cleared his throat. "Mom told me about your outburst and how you really want a Christmas tree. She thought it was okay, but I disagree. The answer is absolutely not."

He continued talking about how Zayde and Baba would be disappointed in us, about how he didn't want our family to cross that cultural line.

Crushed, I fled to my room. Covering my ears with both hands, I tuned out his homily and hurled myself on my bed.

Hanukkah began early December and ended long before Santa Claus slid down my friends' chimneys. We decorated the house with an array of plastic dreidels, blue-and-gold cardboard paper menorahs, as well as brass and silver ones with candles that we lit every night while reciting the prayers. My parents gave me So Big, a life-sized doll I'd been coveting for months, but rather than jump up and down, I held onto my disappointment.

Since we didn't get a sapling, I helped my best friend and her family with theirs, carefully attaching Santa on skis, little wooden wreaths, delicate clip-on birds, and colored glass sphere ornaments. Her mother let us drape plastic silvery strands of tinsel over each branch. Stroking the limbs, I inhaled the pine forest smell, longing for my own, sensing I would/could/should never ask for one again.

Shaped,
San Francisco Bay Area,
1970-80s

After a decade at the Conservative Temple Beth Abraham, we switched to the Reform Temple Isaiah, where several of my parents' U.C. Berkeley sorority sisters and fraternity brothers already belonged.

While my parents continued to model religious and communal leadership, serving on committees and boards, ■ and I attended Hebrew School and temple youth group activities like Purim carnivals and Shabbaton sleepovers. The summer before ninth grade, I befriended Reform Jews from northern, southern, and central California at camp. The next summer, I spent six weeks in Israel with my confirmation class. Throughout high school, I served on the Reform movement's regional and national boards, attending weekly meetings in San Francisco and a conference in Washington D.C. As Chaplain, I organized and led Shabbat services during weekend retreats.

Reform Judaism—the movement, its message of acceptance of all Jews, the equality between the sexes—molded me into the Jew I became by the time I met Mari.

When our rabbi asked us confirmands: "What are you—your nationality, religion, or gender?" I'd formed my answer: female, American, Jew.

reflexionem

In the hills outside of Jerusalem, I join a group of English-language writers at a workshop on reflection. The mid-September sun is so ferocious, so unforgiving. Green abounds: pendulous trees, wild cacti, fragrant flowers.

Sherri Mandell, author of *The Blessing of a Broken Heart* about losing her son to terrorism and grief, explains the workshop falls between Rosh Hashanah and Yom Kippur, called the Days of Awe, because it's a time for thoughtful reflection. Explains its etymology from Late Latin reflexionem, a reflection, or literally a bending back. Explains reflection is to bend back, to stop and look back, to double check yourself.

"While action and description tell the story, reflection is how a writer negotiates it," Sherri says. "The story's the surface, but then bend yourself, bend your story back to see how you relate to it because there's something behind."

My brain and body fasten together like a seatbelt. My two separate identities—my yogi and writer selves—

Jennifer Lang

become one. On the mat, I draw my shoulder blades towards one another to open my chest, to lift my heart. At my desk, I lean forward to write, to make meaning of my life. Was anyone to ask the centuries-old, philosophical "who are you?" I'd answer: a back bender.

During my drive home, I replay her words, convinced they are a sign.

Master of Fine Arts

Late one night, I plop on the bed and glare at Mari. Both my yoga studio and my writing classes have been emptier than usual.

"I miss my old life, where I felt fulfilled professionally. I miss people who knew me outside this cloistered Jewish bubble." I pause. "I'm different from most Anglos who choose to be here, who love this land unconditionally, as if they've been brainwashed."

Sometimes when I meet friends, mostly Anglophones or Francophiles, all new immigrants, each convinced Israel is better for their kids/husbands/themselves, convinced Israel is for every Jew, convinced Israel can do no harm, I feel lonely.

He kisses my lashes, my lips. "Maybe it's time to go back to school."

School, as in an MFA in writing, one of many topics that arose with a therapist we'd started seeing after our Year of Living Differently, when Mari and I stood on opposite sides of our family's fence and she'd asked what I needed to contemplate this move.

"You think the girls could handle my absences?" I ask, even though sometimes I feel obsolete.

If given the chance, Mari would opt for primary house husband over primary breadwinner. He does everything but laundry: gardener, pizza maker, challah baker.

He nods. I notice how round his face has become with age.

The next day, I research low-residency programs in America where students spend intense chunks of time on campus and work one-on-one with a mentor online at home. Most take two years. It means flying west every six months and immersing for 11 days. I apply to Vermont College of Fine Arts, attracted by its summer option in Slovenia. But aside from my spouse, I keep it to myself lest I jinx my luck. Ever since our year in Israel, I'd become very superstitious.

Whenever anyone asks what's new, I simper.

בית ריק

In the security line at Ben Gurion Airport, Mari and I smother the girls with farewell hugs and bon voyage kisses before their flight to San Francisco to see my parents.

Daughter #2 puts hands on hips and says with adolescent sass, "No fair! You guys never go away and leave us a bayit rek."

"Bayit" means house and "rek," empty; together they form an idiomatic expression to mean parents away, kids party.

"You got that right," I say.

Where we live, disquiet gurgles beneath the surface. The politics—and level of security—can flip overnight. I am not ready, and the girls are not old enough to be alone if The Situation were to heat up suddenly. Mari and I are.

During our two-week hollow house, we dine at an upscale Italian restaurant in Tel Aviv. Meander through the Carmel market and the old Yemenite neighborhood. Invite friends for an end-of-summer party. See *We're the Millers* at 10:00 p.m. Traipse around the house naked.

"I kind of like this," Mari says. "Do you think it'll be this much fun after they really leave?"

Our emptiness lets us glimpse our not-so-far-off future. But in Israel, kids leave home a lot later, particularly those who adhere to the typical trifecta: army, trip, college.

I shrug, unable to commit, because all I can think about is if the kids leave the country, why would I stay?

Yes

When the acceptance email from Vermont College of Fine Arts chimes in my inbox, I yell through the house, "I got in! They said yes! I'm going!"

Half Moon Pose

While introducing myself to Shani's students, my voice cracks like a 13-year-old boy's. All week, I couldn't stop thinking about our different teaching styles. She sticks to the set sequence of poses in the Ashtanga series; I go-with-the-Vinyasa flow, mixing and matching so no one anticipates what's next. She keeps personal anecdotes off the mat; I use them to distract my students. She speaks more monotone, while my pitch crescendos.

When Shani asked me to sub, we discussed everything from keys to fees, overlooking language. My stint at Ella hadn't lasted long enough for me to overcome the Hebrew hurdle. She had no idea how much translation rattled my brain. But if she considers me capable, maybe I am.

I usher her students from Triangle into Half Moon. Simple words—left, right, arm, leg, hand, foot—aren't the issue. With one hand on the floor for stability and the top leg lifted, I tell them to tilt their thighs.

A united giggle fills the studio.

"You mix yarech with yareach," a woman says, emphasizing the missing vowel.

My cheeks burn. Meant thighs, said moons. My inner thermometer stabilizes. Together, we shake with laughter.

In that room, it dawns on me; I can do what Shani assumes, what Mari hopes. With Little-Engine-That-Could authority, I can teach in Hebrew.

In my belly

On a pristine June day, the girls and I brunch outside: not too hot, not too humid, just right. We set the table with Mari's homemade strawberry jam, maple syrup, and Nutella.

"I feel bad, but this feels so normal," I say. They look up, their plates full of French toast with whole wheat challah and toppings. "I grew up eating Saturday morning breakfast in our backyard and miss it."

"I get it," Daughter #1 says. "It's nice. I wish we could do it this way, too."

I gaze at the pool shimmering against its checkered turquoise-teal tiles. Behind stands a handful of scrawny trees. Beyond the shrubs, a concrete wall and slatted fence create a barrier between our house and a vacant lot. Mounds and mounds of dirt fill the vast, open space. Like many places in this country, it's a constant work in progress.

Daughter #2 eyes her plate and moves methodically: smear, cut, bite, chew, swallow. She's a rule follower, like me.

We can't make typical American comfort food on Saturdays because using electricity is one among many Sabbath prohibitions. But while Mari's out of the country, I break the laws, live freely in my house, shed my going-rogue guilt, and tuck the truth in the bottom of my belly.

F-F-F,
New York, 2006

Daughters barged into my bedroom while I was getting dressed. Son galumphed down the stairs.

"On y va," Mari bellowed from the living room.

"Mommy, hurry up. Time for shul. But you can't wear leather shoes," Daughter (#1 or #2?) said.

"Go away!" I barked.

Why wearing leather is prohibited on Yom Kippur riled me. Just because my kids were being taught to believe in and abide by this didn't mean I did too.

In my nuclear family, my parents and I had been expected to accommodate ██'s religion-related wishes to keep the peace. In my marriage, I was expected to accommodate Mari's religion-related wishes to preserve shalom bayit—☮ in the ⌂. But since when did I have to accommodate my offspring?

When had I stopped Flexing my opinions?

Forsaken my selfhood?

Forgotten who I am?

Cultural vertigo

Next in line at Newark International Airport's passport control, I hand the agent my American document: 4:15 a.m. local time. We lock eyes. His are gunmetal gray and lidded, distant and detached; mine, red-rimmed with fatigue after a seven-hour Ambien-induced sleep, four hours of zombie-screen-staring time, and another two until my plane to Burlington, Vermont.

"How long were you in Tel Aviv?" he asks, flipping pages.

No stamp or proof in my document. I use my Israeli one to enter and exit that faraway land.

Words escape, unrehearsed, un-thought-out: "A few months."

I shift my weight, baffled by my impromptu response. Perhaps a fantasy—an unconscious mind game of how I'd answer if I still lived here. (Or is it fear?) (Could he revoke my American ID since I really reside in a different hemisphere?)

"Purpose of your stay?"

His repetitive movement—sliding passport photo page back and forth across scanner—hypnotizes me. I question his question. (Is this extreme jet lag playing tricks on my mind?)

"Pleasure?" I say as if asking instead of answering.

Mr. Official points at a microscopic blinking light, checking my passport photo against voodoo rays, and says, "Look there." (Does cyber recognition know?) (Does he?) (Aren't we all playing roles?) Although I dress the born-in-the-USA part—sweatpants, sneakers, sweatshirt—I have emigrated. (Or is it immigrated?)

"Welcome home," the agent says, handing me my passport.

"Thanks," I say, desperate to believe him.

Child's Pose

I hear every one of the teacher's footsteps. She walks and talks, talks and walks. The Vermont sun hammers the wall of windows. My body is tired and overwrought from the time difference, but my mind is overexcited, pumped from adrenaline after a frenzied day of workshops and panels.

"Try to stop efforting," she says. "Try to let go in Child's pose."

She rubs up and down the length of my spine. The space between me and the ground compresses. I giggle.

"You okay?" she asks.

I sit on my heels. "Sorry," I laugh, my entire body jiggling, an uncontrollable, genetic trait that makes strangers stare.

Before class, I introduced myself, telling her about my MFA program, about my goal of writing a book. "See if you can breathe."

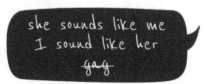

she sounds like me
I sound like her
~~gag~~

From Balasana, she instructs us to take one step forward at a time and hang over our legs, unfurling our spine, to stand. On my feet, I survey my surroundings. Outside is Main Street, Montpelier's primary thorough-fare, smiling like a Norman Rockwell painting: the red brick firehouse with two gleaming engines, the local pharmacy with its Christmas-colored awning, the hole-in-the-wall candy store. Couples saunter by holding hands; friends converse on the sidewalks; children lick ice cream cones. Beyond the capital's downtown, I gape at the expanse of verdant mountains.

Here only 48 hours, I've already forgotten how far I've traveled, everything and everyone I've left behind.

When the teacher's maternal voice says, "Here, in this room, can you loosen?" I know her words are aimed at me.

Bifurcated II

Midway through my residency, I call our Israeli land-line during a workshop break. Daughter #1 answers with a huff.

"What's wrong?" I ask.

"They found the boys. Dead."

"How do you know?"

"It's everywhere: Facebook, Twitter, Times of Israel, WhatsApp."

With her brother in the army and her induction date set for the subsequent summer, she grasps the implications. Quick comebacks and fast thinking have never been one of my assets. How to respond? I'm sorry, or wish I were there—even if untrue?

"Tell me what else is going on. What did you do today?"

"Went to Jaffa with a friend. Walked along the port and around the flea market, ate falafel. It was super fun, until now."

I peer out the window. A charged sigh escapes. My eyes moisten. The push-me-pull-me between home in America and home in Israel tugs.

We blow kisses. I slog two sets of stairs to the room. Clench a tissue, cover my face. My hands shake. A cavernous sob erupts.

"Are you okay?" strangers ask. "What's wrong?"

"These three Israeli Jewish boys were kidnapped before I left home. Netanyahu accused Hamas. Hamas denied it."

Dozens of eyes stare at me. They've never heard of these boys.

"My daughter told me they were found dead. Netanyahu vows severe retaliation."

Their faces are blank. They have no idea what retaliation means in this region, where everything's fair game: missiles, suicide bombings, knifings, car rammings. Where the biblical eye-for-an-eye bullshit reigns. Where violence knows no end.

I picture myself on my yoga mat, my legs spread apart in Standing Straddle pose—one foot there, the other here—and feel yawning, irreparable pulls between them.

The F bomb

The night after I return from Vermont, a siren screeches, leaving me dumbfounded. The next day, another one. Initially, I thought they were random rockets but now realize they were directed strikes, guided missiles to scare innocent citizens. While the alarm yowls in Raanana, I think what the f***? Since when are Hamas' weapons, situated 60 miles south in Gaza, long-range or powerful enough to reach us in the center of this paltry piece of land?

Mari, the girls, and I scamper downstairs to the basement and file into our safe room, leaving the door slightly open for oxygen. The absence of our soldier makes my bones ache.

"You okay?" I ask.

I'm definitely not

The girls nod, wordless, seemingly unfazed. My mind torments me with unanswerable questions and unsettling thoughts: did Son hear the same siren? Did he have time to find shelter? Since he's in an Intelligence unit, did he know Hamas would aim missiles all over the country, a retaliation for the murder of a teenage Palestinian boy after the kidnapping and killing of those three Israeli Jewish boys? When will this chapter end?*

Minutes later—five, maybe ten—we eye each other. "That it?" Daughter #2 asks. "Can we go now?"

Mr. Seer says yes. I open the door, lead us into my darkened yoga studio and up the stairs toward the light.

* January 2024, how naïve I was, we all were.

Meaningless

As soon as I hear the eerie noise, I holler "Siren, come, now!"

Mari and I trot downstairs to the safe room and close the door. Daughter #1 is on a one-month medical volunteer program in Africa and #2, with her grandparents in France. Never have I been more relieved to send them abroad. Hamas had been firing rockets into the south for weeks, but Operation Protective Edge only took effect once missiles began landing near us, near Tel Aviv.

Today's tally: day 𝍸 𝍸

"I never signed up for this," I say. "I warned you that I'd take the kids and go—even if you insisted on staying—if war broke out."

But my threat's meaningless. We both know it. I can't leave while Son—and the sons and daughters of my friends, cousins, neighbors, countrymen—are serving in the IDF. Son finishes in six weeks, but that's never seemed so far away. Plus, no one's calling it war.

Mari kneads his chunky hands into my shoulders. My torso lurches forward. A moan escapes. He enfolds me in his arms. The siren stops. A sizable boom shakes the walls. Like the windows of our house, I shudder.

Conceal, Israel, 1990

At the end of a mild winter's day, Mari and I strode to Mercaz HaCarmel to see *Dances with Wolves* at the theater.

"This country scares me sometimes," I said, unprovoked.

As much as I loved sharing Haifa's beach, souk, universities, and malls with its mixed populations— Jews, Arab Muslims, Arab Christians, Druze, and Bahai—our microcosm of coexistence couldn't conceal the mounting political tension.

The First Intifada or Palestinian uprising against the Israeli occupation of the West Bank and Gaza began before I arrived and dominated newspaper headlines. Every day in ulpan, we learned ugly words like:

funeral	הַלְוָיָה
ammunition	תַחְמוֹשֶׁת
checkpoint	מחסום

Mari grabbed my hand. "But do you get that more people die in car accidents than in terrorist attacks?"

A man of science, he reasoned with facts, numbers, and statistics.

"Maybe. But that doesn't affect how I feel or help me forget what's happening around us."

"I understand," he said, pulsing my palm.

I zipped my coat. "Whenever we were leaving for a trip to Israel when I was little, my parents' friends always asked why, urging us to wait until it was calmer, safer. My parents told them that you can't live your life out of fear or you won't live at all. But I don't know if I can live here long-term. If I can handle the constant stress."

I thought about the irony between Haifa's sluggish pace and the country's fiery ambiance.

"I understand," he said again. "But I don't see it the same way."

Which made me wonder: what do we see the same way?

Class starts late. Everyone's skittish, especially me.

"It's hard to focus, but let's try. Sit tall. Breathe through your nose. In and out. Then inhale for OM," I say.

Some students opt in; several opt out. It took me a decade to feel comfortable uttering the mystical syllable. Year after year, class after class, I vacuum-packed my lips. Did the ancient Sanskrit letters—a - oo – m | அ-உ-ம் | dating as far back as 1200 BCE—mean anything beyond the universal sound, a vibration, to others? So complicated for me. So close to the foreign language of prayer in my religion. So similar to amen.

Eventually, I started chanting it after an Anusara instructor pumped his accordion box and led us in three consecutive rounds, creating a harmonious wave that made my throat constrict, after he described it as "This eternal word is all—what was, what is, and what shall be."

In my studio, I ponder how we practice when we harness control over our mental fluctuations. When we try to change our thoughts and patterns. When we accept that our attitude towards events/objects/ people is what binds or frees us, not the events/objects/

people themselves. When we recognize that the biggest hindrance to our personal development is our own perspectives and prejudices.

A siren pierces the air. We dash into the shelter, where my students frantically dial children and spouses and wait until we hear a far-off, muted boom. After several sirens over the past weeks, we know either a missile has landed or the Iron Dome has felled it, causing fragments to fall from the sky. The loud boom indicates it's safe. The danger has passed.

I open the door. We return to our mats. No one speaks. It's difficult to assume the teacher's role, but these women expect me to lead them, to help them experience the magical mind-body connection of this 5,000-year-old practice. We sit, facing each other, and close our eyes.

In Sanskrit, yoga means yoke: the union of the individual spirit with the universal spirit. How apt to teach it here, where the personal is forever entangled or yoked with the political. Where hamatsav/The Situation is every citizen's birthright.

But just because I was certified to teach, what right did I have to tell anyone in this room to soften, certainly not after sending their son or daughter to their army unit or their spouse to reserve duty?

I slug air. "Inhale for ॐ—the lulling sound representing every sound."

As we join in the three-part A-U-M, I feel the vibration pass from the back of my throat to the tip of my lips and push away the rest.

90 Seconds to Shelter

If an air raid siren didn't clang and I didn't have to run for cover then I would:

1. Ignore news headlines on CNN.com: Israel this, Hamas that, America says, UN accuses
2. Lather shampoo and rinse hair
3. Guzzle eight-ounce glass of water
4. Daydream of Son in civilian clothes in lieu of khaki green IDF uniform
5. Sort laundry: whites, darks, colors
6. Brush teeth
7. Microwave bowl of oatmeal, sprinkle cinnamon, pour milk
8. Boil kettle for cup of Earl Grey tea
9. Measure detergent for washing machine, set timer, turn on
10. Floss
11. Toss pillows on bed
12. Put soap in dishwasher, press start, listen to it purr
13. Fasten earrings, necklace, watch
14. Guzzle eight-ounce glass of water

15. Uninstall the Red Alert app, which indicates where missiles are falling and sirens are ringing throughout the country
16. Moisturize arms and legs
17. Transfer laundry to dryer
18. Lie down, close eyes, do three-part yoga breath
19. Add mango, lychee, pomegranate, and water-melon to WhatsApp family grocery list
20. Delete pictures of Son in army fatigues, bullet-proof vest, and Uzi slung over shoulder
21. Flow through one Sun Salutation in yoga
22. Compose shitty first sentence of new story
23. Fantasize about buying new shoes on Zappos
24. Calculate best time to phone parents ten hours behind in California
25. Microwave leftover pesto pasta for lunch
26. Dismiss news headlines on timesofisrael.com: Gaza this, Israel that, Abbas claims, Netanyahu barks
27. Fantasize about an easier life in America where Amazon and Zappos deliver to your door
28. Download Anthony Doerr's *All the Light We Cannot See* onto Kindle
29. Guzzle eight-ounce glass of water
30. Leave brief message for Son: *hi, how are you, I'm thinking of you*
31. Remind daughters to empty dishwasher and set table for dinner
32. Binge on a half a bar of 66% Lindt dark chocolate

33. Attempt to read girls' report cards in Hebrew
34. Fantasize about an easier life in America where everyone speaks English
35. Give up trying to read girls' report cards in Hebrew
36. Dice clove of garlic, peel ginger, measure soy sauce
37. Stand on one leg in Tree Pose
38. Check phone for message from Son
39. Switch legs in Tree Pose
40. Sip a glass of Ella Valley Cabernet Sauvignon
41. Bathe salmon in teriyaki marinade
42. End dinner table conversations about Iran's nuclear bomb or Hamas' tunnels
43. Check phone for messages
44. Promise to call parents more often
45. Check phone again
46. Copy and paste teachers' comments into Google Translate and laugh at the absurdity
47. Retrieve Son's message of *hey, okay, yah*
48. Pour a second glass of wine
49. ~~Rejoice~~ Regret decision to return to Israel

Ceasefire

Late August, on the 50th day of Operation Protective Edge, Israel and Hamas agree to an open-ended cease-fire brokered by Egypt.

That night, Mari and I throw a joint 98th birthday party to each celebrate turning 49, his belatedly and mine imminently.

Our backyard fills with old friends from our Haifa years along with new friends from France, America, England, Australia, South Africa, and Canada.

Nobody toasts the end of the operation. Nobody believes this ceasefire will stick. Nobody supports the government leaving Gaza with suspected tunnels of terror underneath us. Nobody asks how summer was. Everyone is raw.

Unlike those who witnessed death or lost homes or spent days in shelters, too terrified to leave, we are in one piece. Our anguish pales compared to the loss of a child or of a teen recruit or of a civilian in the wrong place at the worst time.

But we know this incessant madness will detonate again in 12 or 24 months, until the end of time, and that reality seems too heavy, too much to bear.

Am Yisrael—the people of Israel—will march on, but, unlike so many Israelis who were born and raised here, who have lived through decades of war, the sentiment יהיה בסדר does not resonate with me. Never has. Never will. Everything is not okay. It is not f***ing going to be okay. Ever*.

* January 2024, almost a decade later, and this still rings true.

Restless

One sweaty Saturday afternoon, Mari and I stretch out on opposite ends of the sienna-red L-shaped sofa to read. The girls are with friends. Minutes later, he snores. My tolerance time bomb discharges. I wake him up in exclamation points.

"Shabbat bugs the shit out of me! I can't do this anymore! I love Friday nights and family dinners, but Saturday kills me! Nothing but chirping birds, rumbling cars, screeching children! All week long, I spend hours on my ass at my desk, sometimes never leaving the house! Come Friday and Saturday, I need a break!"

He stares at me.

"My phone stopped ringing months ago. Some days, the only people I see are yoga students. Aside from my shrinking social circle, I'm still spooked, afraid to go out because I don't trust Hamas or Israel." I stop to breathe. "At least the writer's life suits me. But because downstairs is Sabbath-observant space, I can't even listen to music, watch a movie, or bake cookies today."

Mari is open-eyed and stupefied.

"Remember when you said you felt dead as a Jew in White Plains? Well, that's how I feel every Saturday morning."

In 2010, during one of our more charged therapy sessions, he told me what I'd suspected but had never heard him say. Have we swapped places? Does my discomfort here equal his there?

While the majority of Raanana's residents are secular, everyone slows down or stops on the Sabbath.

"If I make plans to do something and skip Saturday lunch, I feel guilty, but if I stay here to keep you company, I'm restless."

Once upon a time, I adored reading, playing back-gammon, and making love. But that state of nothing-ness no longer satisfies me. Maybe it's midlife. Time slipping. A grown-up, gnawing fear of missing out. Or maybe it's my own mortality staring at me.

"What do you want me to do about it?" he asks.

I shoulder shrug, letting the tension hang between us like black-out blinds.

But in my head, I do the simple subtraction: $10 - 3 = 7$ [years to go].

Heart Chakra

Whenever Rodney led a chakra practice, I felt my muscles more penetratingly, slept more profoundly. Dare I say the spiritual energy system tamed my Type-A tendencies?

"Ready guys?" he asked. "We're working our way toward Camel pose."

I loved how its Sanskrit name, Ustrasana, sloshed in my mouth but preferred to skip the posture. If the average human head weighed 10 pounds, mine felt 15 when I dropped it back over an arched spine.

Rod folded a blanket in half and instructed us to do the same, pointing out the fringes. We also used blocks, belts, and bolsters. He was meticulous and pedantic about how to fold, where to hold, how to press, when to breathe. Of all the accoutrements, the rope wall, where we occasionally hung upside down and stretched giraffe-neck style, made me squeal like a second grader on monkey bars.

"Here's the thing, sometimes our heart chakra gets blocked. You'll sense it if you battle with loneliness, bitterness, fear, or resentment."

That last "r" word buzzed. My go-to emotion.

Rather than drop my head, I tucked my chin toward my chest. I still couldn't name the poses or explain the chakras but knew how to protect myself.

Year 4: 2011-15

Make this place your ...

In the crowded cultural center in Lod, a mixed Arab-Jewish city 30 minutes south, I find a free seat for a concert sponsored by the American Embassy in memory of American journalist Daniel Pearl, who was kidnapped and killed by terrorists in Pakistan in 2002. The room swells with vim.

Israeli musician David Broza sits on a stool, straps his guitar around his neck, and sings solo in Hebrew, English, and Spanish. He shares stories of his upbringing in Spain, of his grandfather who was an early member of the Arab-Israeli peace settlement Neve Shalom. He introduces Mira Awad, with whom he collaborated on his latest project called East Jerusalem/West Jerusalem. Born of a Palestinian father and Christian Bulgarian mother in Israel, Awad enchants the audience in her many dialects.

Finally, the Jerusalem Youth Chorus—some 20 Palestinian and Israeli teenagers—take centerstage with their American Jewish director. They sing with Broza, with Awad, with Broza and Awad together. They end with "Home": written by Greg Holden and Drew Pearson and originally performed by Phillip Phillips. They add an Arabic and Hebrew twist. Tongue trills, flaps, coils, and curls. Each lyric sprouts holes in my heart:

"If you get lost, you can always be found...

you're not alone...

make this place your...

🏠."

Full Wheel Pose

At 7:30 one Saturday morning, a cloudless day in October, Shani leads an outdoor practice at Hasharon Nature Reserve. We line up our mats single file on the narrow deck of the cliff surrounded by sandy trails and wildflowers. Below lies the Mediterranean Sea, a dull, see-through blue. Sailboats bob. Fishermen wade. Birds caw as they circle above us.

After Bridge pose, Shani helps me drop back into Full Wheel. With her hands on my hips, she roots my legs into the planks of wood. I inhale, lift my chest and arch my head over my spine, extending my arms toward terra firma. I tap the wood; she tugs; I stand. After the third one, I fold forward. I hear every one of my prior yoga teachers telling me to anchor my feet, feel Shani pressing me into the earth. My overcrowded mind empties: chitta vritti nirodhah.

I listen to the peals of man and of nature, a reminder of the overwhelming beauty and the smallness of me.

A passenger in a powered parachute puts his hands in prayer and bows, flying so close it's as if we could touch.

Serve

After the chagim, I begin volunteering at Bayit Shel Benji. Built by a British family in memory of their son who was killed in action during the Second Lebanon War, the house provides refuge for over 300 lone soldiers[19] in combat units every year. Volunteers do everything from cooking to laundry to cleaning. I started volunteering after two fell during Operation Protective Edge.

One Saturday afternoon, a peppy woman with pudgy cheeks leans over the ledge of the front desk and asks me, in red-white-and-blue English, what I do. I close my laptop.

"Answer the phone, buzz in visitors, help anyone who asks. It's four hours, once a month, a great way to spend a Shabbat afternoon. Plus, it beats lying on my sofa."

American born of Israeli parents, she's here for the IDF, serving in Search and Rescue. Founded in 2013, the coed combat unit undergoes extensive training to learn how to respond to atomic, biological, and chemical warfare. They're sent on missions in Israel and abroad to help in natural disaster relief.

Some Saturdays the lobby is placid. Today, girls in holed jeans and boys with black stubble lounge on threadbare sofas, read *HaAretz* newspaper, play piano. A different crowd rolls cigarettes and snaps sunflower seeds outside.

"Nice meeting you," Search-and-Rescue Soldier says, moving the green thumbtack from the in-the-house column to the on-errands column on the bulletin board.

Late tonight or tomorrow morning, she'll likely move it to the last column—on-base—only returning to this home away from home in a couple of weeks.

Tree Pose

Late December, I binge watch four movies on the plane to Vermont for my second semester and arrive numb from fatigue. On day three, I rise early to teach yoga in the chapel of the stately brick College Hall building.

"Brrrr," everyone says upon arrival. The radiators clink like a tired train, struggling to heat the immense room with high ceilings and outdated windows.

"I don't know about y'all, but there's nothing like a residency to make me feel off-balance. So let's try to balance in Tree pose. To do what our body needs but fights," I say to the men and women bold enough to face the icy cold and come to class, catching eyes with my fellow Berkeley-born friend Megan.

Tired nods. Half smiles. An audible groan. Balancing is tricky.

Six months ago, during my first time on campus, I mentioned yoga. My peers expressed interest and the administration granted us this space. Standing in a semicircle on the podium's champagne-colored carpet, I suggest changing positions.

"Find a gaze point. A lot of our ability to stand on one leg starts with our ability to focus. In Sanskrit, it's called drishti."

I wait for everyone to find stillness. Lead them into the pose. The gilded pipes of the floor-to-ceiling organ shimmer behind them. One loses her balance and abandons. The heaters hiss again—clink, clank, clonk.

"Believe it or not, this pose helps calm our minds to relieve anxious thoughts and sentiments. Anyone else anxious sometimes—or am I the only one?"

Before leaving Israel, I couldn't wait to immerse. But since my arrival, I've suffered from jet-lag sleeplessness and fish-out-of-water feelings, unsure with whom to sit in the cafeteria or share summer stories.

"Me too," I hear others say.

Or maybe it's all in my head?

Break free

After the new year, Mari and I spend Shabbat in Haifa
to revisit our old stomping ground. On Friday morning,
we ride the Carmelit funicular to Paris Square and head
straight to the Turkish market. Colorful murals and
splashy street art draw my eye. Red-and-blue Israel
Railway trains, running north to Nahariya and south
to Beersheva, puff into the station. The clement waves
of the Mediterranean hum in the harbor. Mosques with
silver and turquoise painted turrets summon worshippers. Men and women speak Arabic, Hebrew, Russian,
and Amharic on every street.

"Was it like this when we lived here?" I ask.

Mari shrugs.

Haifa in the early '90s was worn out like a retirement
facility, not a hip or happening city.

We hike up steep, decrepit stairs to Hadar in search of
our former spots. Nothing looks familiar, yet everything
looks the same. Orange kiosks on sidewalks sell lottery
tickets and parched-skin men hawk tacky tchotchkes.
Arabs and Jews buy pita from the same bakery and sit
side by side at falafel stands.

"Was it always like this?" Mari asks.

I shrug.

Haifa in the early '90s was the city most likely to sleep through the 21st century.

Holding hands, we brace ourselves for the climb toward our hotel in Mercaz HaCarmel, not far from our newlywed apartment.

"Maybe it's good that some things don't change," he adds.

His words make me wonder. For two decades, I felt trapped in my own story. As protagonist, I'd blabbed to my inner circle about making compromises in a cross-cultural marriage, telling and re-telling my emotional truth, creating my very own personal prison cell. The only way to separate from and move beyond that cell was to own my part, take responsibility, change. I had to grow up and accept that change involved loss and let go. I want to live my life and not the story I've been telling myself and everyone else. I want less angst on the home front—if only I can figure out how to make that happen.

Trikonasana

For the past few months, I've felt antsy, in need of shaking up my routine. Rather than practice the vigorous Vinyasa with Shelley, I've become a fixture at an advanced Iyengar practice with an American teacher. Using the rope walls reminds me of Rodney and Piedmont Yoga Studio.

Someone takes a picture of me with three yogis, each tugging on a strap around distinct parts of my body while pressing me into the wall. I feel the push-me-pull-me sensation in my body akin to Standing Straddle.

Like Humpty Dumpty, I'm being pulled apart and put back together simultaneously. I lean back, confident the wall will steady me, these women will support me, the ground will always be there.

That happened

One spring weekday, I join a bus full of English speakers to drive 60 miles south toward the Gaza Strip. A tour to challenge myself and to see what life under fire looks like. Our escort reviews the rule: if a siren rings, we have 15 seconds to shelter.

At Nitzan, a religious settlement near Ashkelon, we visit a museum and listen to residents of the former bloc of Jewish settlements in the southern Strip, dismantled by the IDF in 2005 as part of Israel's unilateral disengagement from the disputed area. We watch footage of the military forced to usher 8,600 residents out, pain and tears visible on everyone's faces.

At Sderot, a small city less than a mile from Gaza and often a major target of Qassam rocket attacks, we meet the head of a nonprofit serving children of single-parent homes, Holocaust survivors, the elderly, and victims of terror. Last summer, throughout Operation Protective Edge, she and her husband debated whether they should stay or go, their six-year-old son too scared to use the bathroom by himself. They stayed to show solidarity. At the police station, we stand in the volcanic heat taking pictures of deadly metals—missiles, shrapnel, mortar, and Iron Dome fragments—that have fallen from the sky, each one tagged with date, location, impact.

We end at Moshav Netiv Ha'asara[20], where a resident explains the challenges of raising children in a community striving for normalcy under fire and tells us we hear Hamas' training camps beyond the border. We face south: their greenhouses growing flowers and produce for European export; an entrance to a tunnel that was uncovered and destroyed this past summer; a nine-foot concrete wall separating Gaza from Israel. Every inch of cement is covered with vibrant mosaic tiles in the shapes of butterflies, stars, and seashells to make the divider less frightening, to beautify the words Netiv L'shalom or Path to Peace.

On the bus, I keep to myself, buried in thoughts: about how some choose the tougher path, about how others are stuck, like in Syria, about how Carolyn Forché's witness poetry asks its readers to recognize "that which happened." Mostly I think about how privileged I am to have options and how living in this mercurial sliver of land makes me bear witness again and again and again.

Pine

The girls arrive after school hot and bothered and hungry, in need of nourishment.

"Ohhhhh," Daughter #1 says, eyeing their cousin's bat mitzvah invitation. Last year, we missed one in Philadelphia, this year in San Francisco. Every time these glossy save-the-dates arrive 365 days in advance and those family events approach, I feel a pang.

"She's so cute. Please," she presses palms together, plasters on bunny eyes.

"Let me see," Daughter #2 says then seals her sentiments inside like Mari.

We can't go because Memorial Day weekend is end-of-school-year-test-crunch time for them and last-packet-MFA-crunch time for me. But I can imagine the scene: my parents, aunt and uncle, cousins and kids in dressy clothes to pose for pictures at a Friday night dinner, sit together during Saturday morning services, give speeches at lunch, dance the Hora at a party, and gorge on Sunday brunch of eggs benedict and bagels. And all the becauses and buts blindside me every time.

"I know we can't," says Daughter #1 as if to comfort me. "I get it."

Barrier, New York, 2010

Lately, the main topic in couples' counseling was what I'd miss most if we moved to Israel.

"My list is long," I said. "Besides my yoga and writing communities, there's the library, Netflix, and Whole Foods." My voice trailed off with fatigue and longing—or perhaps resignation?

"Buy a Kindle," Mari said. I knew every branch in every city, town, and village throughout Westchester County; an electronic reading device could never replace my weekly stops at the ivy-and-brick Scarsdale Library. "The kids can show you how to pirate movies, or we'll get a proxy."

Utterly illegal, unethical, immoral. I glanced at the trees on Mamaroneck Avenue.

"What else?" the therapist asked.

"The change of seasons." In the Bay Area, I'd never paid attention to them, but living in the Northeast had heightened my awareness and appreciation. "My parents, growing old alone."

"Keep going."

"Our girls," I said, my shoulders shaking, "feeling jilted like it's about their brother. Leaving an American education like it doesn't matter. Serving in the army like they have no say."

She jotted notes, perhaps writing "they're screwed" or "poor kids."

I wrenched another Kleenex.

"What do you have to say to your wife?"

Mari swiveled in my direction. "I know you don't want to leave, and it's hard for you in Israel sometimes. But can we think about this seriously? For us?"

Aware of every sentence starting with but, I thought about my aunt, who'd called recently and said, "Gee, honey, you sure have a lot of drama in your life."

I thought about that drama and about how much I wanted to make it disappear, about how we were our biggest barriers and about how we got in our own ways, about how much I wanted to get out of mine and about how every therapy session and thought process kept coming back to choice.

Unaccompanied minors, New York, 2006

Every summer since Son and his sisters turned six, we placed powder blue UM—unaccompanied minor—pouches around their necks, snapped pictures with their bloated backpacks, and stifled them with parental love before watching them step through security toward their overnight flight to Frankfurt. Every summer, they spent quality time with their French grandparents to learn the language, values, and customs. It was both a privilege and a price of being part of a bicultural family.

But September 11th had changed the landscape, challenged our decisions. In 2006, I lost sleep between the British government divulging a plot intended to destroy transatlantic aircraft mid-flight using explosives in the suspects' hand luggage and the IDF and Hezbollah paramilitary forces waging war in northern Israel. All summer, friends asked if we were still going to celebrate Son's bar mitzvah, if we had a back-up plan in case it continued.

Stress squatted in my body. To relax, I tried kick-ass yoga classes and fast walks. I wrote endless lists: school supplies to buy, books to pack, friends to call. Lists made me feel a false sense of control.

Like Arthur Krystal writes in *The Joy of Lists:* "... there is something reassuring about a list, a precision and formality that makes us think we've got a handle on things. Isn't every list in reality a ceremonial flourish against amnesia and chaos?"

"The war will be over by the time we go," Mari said.

How I despised this spousal dynamic. Where he saw himself as invincible, where he downplayed my fear, where he could never step into my shoes, where I curbed my words. When my throat chakra was suppressed and achy.

Signs

After three email inquiries about creative writing classes, I perform an uneducated cost-benefits analysis: do the pros of teaching outweigh the cons? Do I have a vast enough network to start my own classes? That same week, three more people express interest.

Along with superstition, I believe in signs. Signs that come from the universe. Signs that connect me with my desires. Signs that validate my direction and decisions.

Convinced, I start Israel Writers Studio and smear it on Facebook. A smatter of people register for JUST WRITE!

I set my dining room table with painted wooden placemats. Fill my grandmother's floral teapot with Earl Grey. Introduce them to narrative arc, the most befitting starting point, to begin our journey.

Low Lunge Pose

Every Tuesday, we squish mat to mat in Herzlia's WeWork boardroom, wallpapered with images of skyscrapers, a patchwork of primary colors. I bark orders like an IDF commander: right foot forward, left foot back, left knee down, arms up, fingers spreading.

"I would have liked the army," I say.

Those who understand, giggle. Someone utters "oy" under his breath. Another says "maniyak," a common Anglicized slang word I take as maniacal. I hear grunting.

"It's one thing to be in the pose, but it's another to loosen while you're in it. Can you try?"

Another oy. Another grunt. I muse on the mythology behind the pose—how Anjaneyasana is named after Anjana, the mother of Hanuman, often called a monkey and considered the superhero of the epic Ramayana tale; how she was thought to be a powerful practitioner, performing tapas[21] to control the mind, body, and senses.

"Sure, sure, whatever you think. Enough!" a jokester says.

He releases the posture, and everyone topples like a game of dominos.

Mid-century

At summer's end, for our 50th birthdays and 25th wedding anniversary, Mari and I leave the girls with friends and escape to Santorini. For seven straight days, we dunk in Greekdom. We hike from the village of Fira to the northern tip of the island at Oia to watch the famous sunset. We rent an All-Terrain Vehicle, and with my arms draped tightly around Mari's thickening waist, we explore wineries and excavations. We snap endless photos: white adobe houses and azure blue roofs, stubborn donkeys, breathless cliffs. Israel is far from my thoughts; aside from my kids, I don't miss anything. On our last morning, we take a stand-up-paddle board lesson.

"Can you do this?" Mari asks, attempting to lift one leg before tipping into the flat Aegean Sea.

Slowly, I lift my butt into Downward Facing Dog then place one foot forward and open my arms into Warrior II before landing in the water. We chuckle like schoolchildren.

Every day, I study my husband: how his face crinkles when he smiles, how his feet have suntanned strap marks from his sandals, how his bald head shimmers with sweat. I see the young man with the impish grin is still there.

But am I?

Throat Chakra

After Camel pose, I thought the remainder of class would be easy. Wrong.

"We're almost done. Only three more chakras to go. Next one is the throat," Rodney said.

In Child's pose, my body curled into itself, I inhaled the scent of Chez Simone's cinnamon sweet apple tart.

"Think of the chakras like this. All day, we pick up vibes from the people around us. Their vibes clog our systems. Chakras work like car filters. They clean out excess garbage and make space for what you need. When not working properly, though, they get blocked."

He recited frequent physical symptoms of blockage: chronic sore throat (N/A), frequent headaches (N/A), and thyroid issues (N/A). But then he added hoarseness/laryngitis, dental issues, and neck pain: all applicable. How could I distinguish between motherhood-related stress, marital stress, work-family-juggle stress, and throat chakra blockage?

"Then there are the non-physical signs of blockage. Like fear of speaking, inability to express thoughts, keep secrets or keep your word." Cold shower shivers covered my body. "Energy that flows freely through the throat promotes effective, truthful communication. That means you need to work through and shuck off emotions like guilt, hurt, and resentment."

Could crying count as a cleanse, as freedom of the fifth chakra?

He instructed us to lie on our bellies, bend our knees and grab our ankles in Bow pose. As I lifted my legs and upper body off the floor, my chest zinged. Open and alive.

"Think of this as the place where we speak our authentic voice," Rod said. "Where impulse turns into choice and action. Because when it's open and stimulated, your voice moves through space to help you communicate your emotions in healthy ways. Can you ask for what you need?"

Could I?

Year 5: 2015-16

Status quo

Between Rosh Hashanah and Yom Kippur, I fly to California to see my parents. During my first week, I accompany my mother to her therapy session. When this stranger asks what we want to discuss, my mother plows forward with her typical he-this, he-that refrain.

He = my father.

We sit a few feet apart on the itchy sofa.

"Actually, something's on my mind," I interrupt.

Both women glue their eyes on me.

I face my mother. "Status quo with you and Dad isn't working. Something's gotta give."

Despite oceans between us, we see each other several times a year. Visits are intense. The room hushes. I hear every passing car.

"What do you think?" the therapist asks.

My mother looks at me, at her lap. "What exactly do you propose?"

I'm armed with ideas. "You call it quits after 59 years." She stiffens. "Or move to Israel. We're all there." The global "we" grows every year as ██'s children marry and start families. "We find a full-time caregiver for Dad so you can travel. If you move nearby, I can help with doctors, hairdresser, gym. Think about the alternative. Do you really want to do this getting older thing here, alone?"

Since I arrived, she's told me about so-and-so's cancer diagnosis, so-and-so's move closer to their kids, and so-and-so's new retirement community.

In a surprisingly gentle tone, my mother says, "I'll think about it."

More headlines

Throughout my visit, my parents are consumed by the most recent outbreak of violence over the Temple Mount in Jerusalem. Over Saturday morning fried eggs and mixed berries, I watch the sun fence with the fog outside the bay window.

"I can't believe how crazy they are!" my mother says, reading the front page of the *San Francisco Chronicle.*

It's unclear if 'they' refers to Israeli Jews or Palestinians or journalists.

"Yeah, it's always the same story," my father says, clutching *The New York Times,* which he reads and rereads since he's unable to retain new information.

Alzheimer's aside, he's got that right. Some say tension started in September when Israeli soldiers killed a Palestinian woman at a checkpoint in Hebron on her way to school; others say it began earlier, on Rosh Hashanah eve, when Israeli police raided the plaza outside al-Aqsa Mosque, firing rubber-coated bullets and throwing stun grenades toward Palestinian youths barricaded inside and hurling rocks and flares. Perhaps it began in July when Israeli settlers firebombed a house in Duma, killing three Palestinians.

No one asks my opinion. That trouble started before the Bible was written or even called the Bible in this land of milk and honey, of love and hatred. That boundary between start and finish, war and peace has blurred into oblivion.

"You done yet?" she asks him.

He sets down his cappuccino cup, smacks his lips with a "Sure," and switches papers.

T-0

For my last weekend, I fly to Los Angeles to see close friends, each of whom shares their favorite haunt. Today is Will Rogers State Historic Park near Pacific Palisades.

"You ready to go back?" my hostess asks.

"That's loaded. I miss the girls but know they're fine, especially with you know who. Sometimes he's more present, more patient than me."

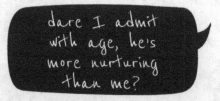

"And do you miss your husband?"

"I do—and I don't."

"I miss being with him but wish he wasn't, as in we weren't, there, in Israel, so far away. Despite my parents' messy history, it's getting harder and harder to say goodbye. And every time I drive or shop at Trader Joe's or Target, I'm struck by American easiness, manners, and niceties. Then there's the San Francisco skyline at night, the Golden Gate peeking through clouds."

Accustomed to these hills, she walks without panting. Fast walking in Raanana is flat. Driblets of sweat swim on my forehead. I feel dizzy.

"And what do you think about the whole Temple Mount story and the stabbings? Does that make you want to stay here too?"

My eyes well. Only old friends get to the heart of difficult discussions so quickly.

"Yep," I say. "The news makes me want to stay. But what? I stay here and leave my kids and husband there?" I gesture: one palm face down on top of another for time-out.

"Need water."

I gaze east at the colossal SoCal houses to one side and the sweeping Pacific Ocean to the other and suck in air, crouch low to the ground, close my eyes, and beseech the earth to stop spinning.

Renege

In the boarding area of LAX, I call my mother before my 14-hour trip to Tel Aviv.

"Remember last week when we discussed changing the status quo?"

"Of course. I lost sleep again last night thinking about it."

"Yeah, same. I can't promise you that I'll be there." A pity party of tears gushes. "I dread going back to the stabbings, to Daughter #1 going into the army, wearing a uniform, taking a bus. I don't know what the future will bring."

Our trip to Santorini was only one month ago but seems like a different century.

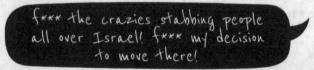

"I appreciate your offer. My therapist made me appreciate how lucky I am to have you, but I don't want to leave here or live there. I never have."

When the airport staff announce boarding time, we swap "I'm sorry"s and "I love you"s and "see you soon"s and hang up, and I trudge toward the plane.

Reneger, Israel, 2010

(n.): a person who reneges
(pron.): me

At the end of our summer in Israel, the day after telling our tween and teens our decision to return permanently the following summer, I reneged, admitting I couldn't do it, leaving Mari stony and speechless.

Cocktail,
Israel, 2010

Twenty-four hours before reneging, Mari and I indulged our children in Dr. Lek's mint chocolate chip gelato.

"What's the occasion?" Son asked.

"Big news," Mari said.

Everybody looked at each other.

"What? What now?" Daughter #2 asked.

Last time we'd shared big news was winter 2007, during a one-of-a-kind family meeting, when we announced our plan to spend a year in Raanana.

"Well, Mommy and I have agreed . . . at the end of this school year, we're moving back to Israel."

Stupor. Silence. Shock.

"No way!" Son shrieked. "You'll ruin everything. I'm signing up to be a lone soldier but can't if you come too."

Neither Mari nor I had expected this reaction. We hadn't been involved in his army enlistment process, weren't privy to the perks he'd receive (higher salary, shared apartment) if he joined the IDF on his own. The girls, 13 and 11, dissolved in tears. Unlike me, they rarely cried.

"I don't want to live here!" Daughter #1 shouted. "Summers are enough!"

Daughter #2 stomped upstairs, Mari chasing after her.

Daughter #1 flung herself on the living room sofa. "What's the point?" she pleaded. "We did this two years ago: left our friends, moved here, left here, moved back to New York. Why would you make us do that again?"

She expected answers.

An emotional whirlwind swirled inside me. Guilty Mari and I were unable to agree on a country to raise our family. Sorry our children felt rootless. Responsible for their excessive vectors.

"Well," I said, stroking my daughter's hair. "It's אבא's dream. He's always wanted to live here. We're doing this for him. We've been in the States for 15 years, and now I owe him time."

I squeezed next to her. Son hurled himself onto the other sofa. The ice cream melted in their bowls.

"Why are you making us do this again?" she repeated, a scratched record.

Our tears blended together: a chorus of snot.

Vectors, Israel, 2009

During our annual summer trip, I called Judy, the one I missed the most even though we saw each other the least. A pediatrician for the public health clinic, she worked overtime all the time. We made a date to meet at the beach in Herzlia during her limited free time.

"Okay, sweetie, what's your story? What's the Israel status?" she asked.

I told her how therapy helped us rebuild our foundation. How Mari and I wrote long emails to each other while apart this summer. How we still shared an extreme love despite core differences.

"Do you know what a vector is?"

I shrugged.

A science and math major, she explained the fundamentals: a quantity possessing both magnitude and direction, represented by an arrow the direction of which indicates the direction of quantity and the length of which is proportional to the magnitude.

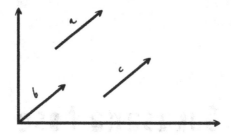

"Your vectors are f***ed up. They're pointing every-where—France, Israel, America—but you need them to point to one place. Like Marcia; hers point to California and her kids are 100 percent American."

Ever since we met at Temple Isaiah Hebrew School, the three of us have been tied together like strands of a rope.

"Mine point to Israel. My kids are 100 percent Israeli. If you don't aim them at the same spot, your kids will end up like you with their vectors in different directions. You have to change your vectors, sweetie. Get it?"

Sukasana Pose

Helicopters hover overhead, low and loud and odd in a city where we rarely hear anything other than birds chirping or cars tooting.

"Come close," I shout above the din. "Leave your mats, sit in a circle, knee-to-knee."

We practice outside on my deck since it's one of those rare, idyllic, temperate October days.

For the past month, low-tech stabbings with household items (think steak knives, screwdrivers, vegetable peelers) have spread from Jerusalem to Afula, Tel Aviv to Dimona. But never in our peaceful, protected city where kids walk to school alone.

Throughout our practice, my neighbor stopped several times to check her phone, text, and return to her mat until divulging breaking news: two stabbings reported in Raanana. One in our vicinity. The shock settles.

A fresh American immigrant whimpers. Mari joins us. My neighbor squeezes my hand. Together, we chant ॐ.

Ripple

On the other side of town, in the social hall of a huge synagogue, gobs of females, ranging from little girl to old lady, swarm like mosquitos. Hebrew, English, Italian, French, and Spanish swish in my ears.

A college-aged coed with a bouncy blond ponytail introduces herself and explains she taught Krav Maga[22] in the army. Using sweeping hand gestures, Coed says the key to our safety is paying attention.

"Do not walk or ride a bike with earbuds. If you listen to music, keep only one in so you can hear around you. If you're at a bus stop, put your phone away and watch around you. Never stand in the bus shelter because if someone tries to knife you and you fall back, no one can help or hear you scream. Stand outside so you can turn and watch who's coming from all sides. If anyone approaches with a knife, yell mechabel, mechabel, mechabel, mechabel and run. Run as fast as you can and call for help."

My body temperature plummets.

"Need a weapon?" Coed demonstrates how to hold a key bow in our palm, tip sticking up between her second and third fingers. "If someone tries to stab you, aim for their eyes." She picks up a purse, whips around, and swings it hard. "Anything works: backpack, branch, rock, water bottle, umbrella, walking stick, selfie stick. If you have it, slam it into them. The terrorist won't be expecting it."

"Oh my god"s ripple throughout the room. The teacher introduces her assistant, a teenager in an umpire's mask and plastic knife in hand.

"A stabber's goal is simple: to stab as many times as possible. We must surprise them and fight back. Watch." She bends one arm, retracts her head like a turtle, swats her free hand at his face, and kicks his groin, shrieking mechabel while fleeing.

A preteen raises her hand: "What should we do if someone approaches from behind?"

Coed turns and the assistant pretend-stabs her in the back. She faces him and repeats the same moves. "Got it?"

We snicker. Because it's funny. Because it's uncanny. Because it's insane.

Route 443

During the height of the stabbings, we dress in our most modest clothes and drive an hour south to Jerusalem, the hotspot of the conflict, for my niece's wedding. Even my parents flew to Israel for the occasion.

At 11:00 p.m., at the end of the festivities, we turn on WAZE for directions and press HOME. When Mari speeds by the turnoff to the main highway, following the phantom companion to 443[23], a busy traffic artery and one of only two highways connecting Jerusalem to Israel's coastal plain along the Mediterranean Sea, I flip.

"Where are you going"? I turn around to see if the girls hear me, but they're already asleep. Oblivious. "I refuse to drive on this road right now!"

Unlike Route 1, it runs through Palestinian areas, in between unfriendly villages that overlook the road from nearby hills.

"It's her fault," he points at his phone propped on a magnetic mount. "She told me where to go."

"She doesn't know any better. She's tied to traffic, not to politics!"

If only we could embody WAZE's ways and live more freely.

Mari clamps the wheel. There's no turning back and changing routes. I want to close my eyes like the girls but keep vigil instead.

> what if a stray bullet hits us like it did Cate Blanchett on a desert road in Morocco in Babel?

Each one of the road's 20.9 miles makes my pulse pound. The moon illuminates one Palestinian village after the next—Qalandia, Bayt Ghur al-Foqa, Khirbat al-Misbah—in the West Bank. I detect minarets, barbed wire, and the wall: a barrier running along the Green Line separating us from them.

He glances at me. "Ça va?"

I glower. Withhold my knee-jerk-no, absolutely-not-okay response. Purse my lips.

In the opaque night, I picture the two of us sitting shoulder to shoulder in a room full of French students discussing The Conflict; then, in our early twenties, I was naïve, sure that the solution was procurable, certain that if we spoke each other's languages, we could resolve our differences.

Now, my chest hurts from holding my breath, only exhaling after soldiers in helmets and bullet-proof vests with Uzis over their shoulders wave us into Israel. Like when I subbed yoga for Shani, I hear Little-Engine thoughts rumble through me only this time they're negative: I don't think I can. I don't think I can. I don't think I can.

Soapbox

A week after my niece's wedding, my mother, ██, and I meet an American Israeli social worker who runs a binational elder-care company. My initiative. Sibling strife aside, we communicate when it comes to our parents and agreed to rendezvous in a residential city halfway between us, in the back room of an uber-kosher café.

The social worker asks each of us to explain why we're here, what our goals are, and how she can help. I'm relieved. Neither ██ nor I is in charge.

My mother begins. Props her elbows on the table. Clasps her hands together. Mounts her imaginary soapbox. Says her husband wronged her for 25 years, and after he confessed, she stayed, but now—Alzheimer's or other—she can barely look at him.

"I want to stay in America, married, but live alone."

My yoga teacher's words—change is the only constant—sing in my ears.

On wheels

With Israeli life-must-go-on stoicism, Mari and I take Tel Aviv by Segway. A belated birthday present from friends. The instructor resembles a GQ model with sculpted shoulders and sun-kissed skin. He explains how to start and stop the two-wheeled, self-balancing machine. I ride sandwiched between the two men, grateful for bodyguards, even though the daily stabbings have dwindled.

"Where do you live?" Model Man asks as we cruise south.

When I tell him, he shakes his head and says "why, why, why," an Israeli wow.

Thanks to Raanana's stabbings, we're on the terror map, a place where no city or citizen wants to appear. We stop for a photo opportunity in front of a whimsical statue of PM David Ben Gurion, known for proclaiming the establishment of Israel and for being the first to sign the Israeli Declaration of Independence in 1948, as well as for practicing yoga, standing upside down on his head, his old-man belly distended and pigeon-gray hair splayed on the sand.

"Did you think about canceling today?" Model Man asks.

Mari answers no; I

suppress my wimpy yes

As we roll toward Jaffa, the southernmost neighborhood with a significant mixture of Arabs and Jews, the Mediterranean glistens like gemstones. Usually, hordes of beach-goers pervade the shore. Usually, oodles of people swim, surf, and stand upright on paddle boards. Usually, the promenade is clogged with foot, bike, and scooter traffic. But tourism tanks as soon as travel advisory warnings go haywire.

"Kol hakavod," Model Man says, giving a 👍.

A red-and-white Magen David Adom ambulance roars down HaYarkon Street, its siren whining in my ears. I try not to jump to conclusions. I try not to fabricate stories in my head. I try to keep my eyes on the water, to welcome the breeze on my back.

Back-up plans

One sun-drenched Saturday, eight hours post-Paris attacks, 20 hours pre-Daughter #1's army induction, we brunch in our backyard. A hoopoe circles above us with its prominent red-white-and-black Mohawk.

"What's our Plan B?" Daughter #2 asks, smearing hummus on challah. "If ISIS gets here?"

We suggest San Francisco, Scandinavia, South America, but she nixes them: wildfires, taxation, corruption.

"We're safer here than anywhere else," Mari says.

Maybe he's right. Despite innumerable enemies, gun laws are strict, streets are safe.

Yet whenever I weigh the pros and cons, home's always heavier.

Is this saudade?

D-day

"Nervous?" I ask Daughter #1.

We stand eye-to-eye, but today she seems taller. With her leggings, Nikes, and up-do, she appears ready for sleepaway camp, not the Israeli army.

"A little, but mostly about what I packed."

I awkward-laugh to cover my apprehension about soldiers being stabbed at bus stops, on buses, in city streets. At Tel Hashomer base, soldiers inspect our identity cards, our belongings, and her bag. We enter a courtyard of chaos: parents, teenagers, soldiers, civilians, grandparents, aunts, uncles, cousins, siblings, and friends stand, walk, sit, shout, hug, cry, talk, take selfies. Everything I missed with Son's send-off. Today, Daughter #2 couldn't miss school, but my in-laws, visiting from France, come. Screens of names and identity numbers flash. Announcements boom over loudspeakers. Families set out yogurt, cucumber-tomato salad, and pita at picnic tables. Cigarette smoke wafts through the morning air.

"Well, that's me," Daughter #1 says when her name appears. "Ready?"

She might be, but I'm not. We amble toward the honking bus. Dewy, sappy teenage girls give last-minute hugs. Most of my friends' sons and daughters have had unparalleled, life-altering army experiences. As difficult as it is to watch my second one go, I trust hers will shift and shape her too.

My father-in-law holds her head and kisses her forehead. My mother-in-law pecks each of her cheeks. Mari recites the Hebrew prayer for safe passage. I whisper in her ear, "Be strong, I love you, be safe" until she leaves.

50

Midstream during her one-month basic training, our soldier calls in tears. Because her gun must always accompany her—even to the toilet—her tendonitis recurred. I ask if she told her commander.

"You don't get it," she says. "They're all 19-year-old recruits, totally incompetent and disorganized. Anyway, yesterday, they woke us at 3:00 a.m. to drive to a shooting range. We got back at midnight. I was desperate to shower, washed my hair in freezing water, went to bed and woke up from the cold. The hygiene's horrible. Someone had lice; they checked 600 girls' scalps, everyone hoping for bugs to be sent home for two days. Oh, and tonight I have guard duty."

She chatters. I listen, unable to fathom shouldering such responsibility. She bawls. At her age, I entered my freshman year of Northwestern University and rushed a sorority, babbling about boys, majors, and the Midwest.

The next morning, I retrieve a missed message: "Learning how to shoot was beyond insane. I got into the bunker with seven others. None of us want to take anyone's life, but because we live in this country, we must know how to aim and pull the trigger so we can kill somebody. It was a very pivotal moment. Okay, so sending lots of love." She smooches the phone.

Baffled, I press play to listen again.

When had she become so brave, so bold, so Israeli?

Mari opens his arms to hold me, saying, "It's a good thing she's in the army and not you."

Since the day we met, this man has cracked me like a code, knowing how to deactivate my overactive mind, my oversensitive buttons. I cackle-cry into his sweatshirt, sure Daughter #1 will survive and thrive.

Revolved Abdomen Pose

In Vermont for my fourth residency, I awaken early to teach yoga in the Chapel. Winter is vicious. We wear long sleeves and several layers. I smile at my regulars like Megan and Cheryl, Amy and Alisa, here every time I teach.

"A few years ago, I read a great piece by Elizabeth Gilbert, the *Eat-Pray-Love* girl, in *Yoga Journal* magazine about her first time in a yoga class, dressed in jeans and a turtleneck on a full stomach. Can you imagine?"

Everyone giggles. Lying on their back with knees bent, they twist right and look left.

"After poking fun at the shrine in this crowded NYC studio and the teacher chanting OM, Elizabeth Gilbert's on her back, like y'all, when she does this same pose Jathara Parivartanasana."

Some shoulders pop off the carpet. Effort is etched across their foreheads.

"And she has this moment of clarity, as if her body is speaking to her, saying hello, it's alive and present and taking notes."

The radiator hisses.

"She has this revelation, aware of how alive her body feels and how much it craves movement."

Clicks: a spine or rib or hip.

"With that, she weeps. Called it a homecoming."

Pot of memories

Back in Raanana, I rifle through Container Store bins in the basement and lug old photo albums upstairs: 1987, when I worked in Paris after college graduation; 1989, when I moved to Israel and met Mari; 1990, when Mari and I married in the Jerusalem hills; 1993, when our baby was born. The living room carpet is littered with decades of regatta blue par avion aerogrammes from friends and family to me and from me to them thanks to many who have returned my mail.

On May 30, 1989, six weeks after I arrived in Israel between a job and graduate school, I filled every line of six silky sheets of weightless paper with words I cannot

relate to or recall writing: "… something has fallen into place and removed me even further from the States. I did not expect that …

I feel like this is a country where one can make a difference and contribute. There is a sense of need here. There's adventure, outdoors, a de-emphasis on materialism and talk of the world because Israel itself is so small."

I described my week, the highs of exploring Jerusalem's back alleys and book shop-cafes and potential career paths. I was so open-minded and unencumbered.

Upstairs in my office, my fingers fly across the keyboard as I recreate scenes from my early years with Mari. At 3:00 a.m., I compose whole sentences, eager for daylight at my desk. Every month, when I submit new chapters, my mentor responds with thought-provoking feedback about narrative memory, sensory detail, and secondary characters.

As I weigh me-then against me-now, revealing game-changing conversations in couples' counseling and difficult decision-making moments, I don't once stop to look forward. Mari gave me permission to write, but no one warns me about the eventual, potential fallout from stirring the pot of memories.

On the verge

During a humdrum week, Son comes for dinner.

"Okay, I'm leaving now," he says.

He stands in our foyer, one hand on the front door, the other in a casual wave, numb to our goodbyes and to my slush. I look at my no-longer-child child: taller than Mari, green-bean skinny, more manly.

"Please one more hug," I beg-cry.

Twenty-two, he is CEO of a fledgling father-son start-up that developed from his pre-army idea. Now, he's moving thousands of miles west to San Francisco to raise funds. I stand on the second step to fully embrace his six-foot-something frame. Of my three kids, he resembles me most with a long, oval face, deep-set hazel eyes, and russet-colored hair.

"Two hands, please," I say, draping the limp one behind my back. "Squeeze." My eyes prickle. Mari and the girls watch me from the sofa. "Okay, go!"

I dash upstairs, flinging myself on my bed like a character in Pedro Almodóvar's *Women on the Verge of a Nervous Breakdown*. The front door clacks. I phone my mother ten hours behind in Oakland, across the Bay Bridge from where he'll land.

"I'm sorry I left you and Dad like that," I whimper. "I'm sorry I moved so far away. Now I know how much it hurts."

Intersection

For the past ten days, during my final MFA residency in Slovenia, we've explored the former Soviet bloc country and its environs, from Soča Valley, which inspired Ernest Hemingway's *A Farewell to Arms,* to Trieste, Italy, where James Joyce lived and Rilke started writing his *Duino Elegies.* Today we're at Hostel Celica in Ljubljana, where I deliver my lecture and fulfill part of my graduation requirement.

When I scan my peers' and faculty's faces, I see 28 friendly eyes. "In *Tell it Slant,*" I begin, "Brenda Miller and Suzanne Paolo write: Unless you exist on an unchartered island—and are never discovered!—the elements of your life are reverberant with historical significance because you live in a communal group whose attitudes and choices are historically shaped. My lecture is 'Collective Memory: The importance of bearing witness in words,' and it's only appropriate that we're in a building[24] that holds so much history the day after Elie Wiesel's death."

I nod at my PowerPoint wingman and point to the screen. We listen to a recording of Adrienne Rich reading "In Those Years."

"Literature is a medium of remembrance. In witness poetry, readers are asked to recognize, at a bare minimum, that which happened."

A volunteer reads the next slide: Carolyn Forché's "The Colonel." My captured audience shifts in their seats. The folding chairs squeak against the golden hardwood floors.

"Our role as writers is to record, to remember, to pass along, to tell the next generation, to prevent the events from being altered or forgotten or denied, and to make something beautiful out of something ugly."

Sunlight infiltrates the room. My cheeks are aglow.

"Many writers address the greater world and find the intersection between personal and political: George Orwell, Jo Ann Beard, James Baldwin, to name a few. I've published stories about the First Gulf War, Oslo Accords, handshake between Arafat and Rabin. We're going to create a timeline."

I show the set-up from Sondra Perl and Mimi Schwartz's *Writing True: The Art and Craft of Creative Nonfiction* and my earliest memory:

Year	Age	Events	External	Internal
1971	almost 6	Apollo 14	1st trip to Israel	Israel foreign like moon

I missed the last month of kindergarten for our family trip to Israel; in class, we had turned our two-story playhouse into a spaceship, cut out eyes and mouths on Safeway brown paper bags to wear over our heads, made PB&J sandwiches wrapped in aluminum foil, climbed to the top story of the playhouse, counted down from ten and launched into space. Flying to Israel on a big jumbo plane reminded me of flying to the moon. Israel was hot and sticky; I couldn't understand anything in Hebrew; my great aunts and uncles smothered me with hugs and strange food—tangy orange juice, jumbo sesame pretzels, tasteless vanilla ice cream; Zayde and Baba bought an apartment in Tel Aviv, facing the Yarkon River and power plant and fields of dirty nothingness; Zayde lifted me in the elevator to press and count in Hebrew together—achad, shteim, shalosh, arba—like our countdown to the moon in school.

As my lecture ends, adrenaline ekes out of me. Everyone claps and whistles and stands to leave, but I can't move.

Farewell

On our last day in Ljubljana, I read the beginning of my memoir-in-progress, the ultimate requirement to graduate. At first, my words wobble. I practice yoga breath and recall my mother telling me to enunciate.

"Chapter one: Derailment

In the parking lot of the guest house in Shoresh, nestled in the Judean Hills, I greeted Gad, my Parisian friend from Chicago, and his friend from engineering school in France.

'Where's your girlfriend?' I asked Mari, while we exchanged the perfunctory French kisses.

'We broke last night,' he said with an adorable grammatical flaw, sexy accent, and mischievous look in his pecan brown eyes.

He was single. I grinned. He blushed. I eyed the rainbow-colored kippa atop his head.

Who was this Frenchman named Mari and just how Jewish was he? I wondered. Based on the head covering, I assumed he observed Shabbat, but his khaki shorts, t-shirt and sandals indicated he and ▮ represented divergent ends of Orthodoxy.

After dinner, the participants discussed the weekly Torah portion and conceivable solutions to the latest Intifada unrest, but I kept quiet, aware of my left-leaning, liberal, open-minded, northern California notions of coexistence, so foreign to the French. Mostly, I yearned to flirt with Mari."

My eyes sting. I finish reading. A thunderous applause humbles me. School is over, but the real work begins.

back-to-back

One hotter-than-hot summer day, while gorging on Shabbat leftovers for lunch, Mari announces, "I'll be working from home as of tomorrow."

"But *I* work from home."

"I told you our lease expired, and we don't have enough money to rent another one."

Days after Son finished his army service, he and Mari created a company, raised funds, purchased a hodge-podge of desks and ergonomic chairs, and commuted to office space in Herzlia Pituach, where all stages of start-ups work alongside Apple, Microsoft, and Dell.

"What's the problem? There's room for both of us."

In our current setup, two matching his-and-hers IKEA desks are back-to-back in my office. I sit for hours, read aloud, plan classes, research topics, and listen to podcasts.

"But I can't share space with you anymore."

I refrain from saying now that I'm a writer. In New York, my yoga and Jewish communities were separate like my family and writing lives here.

"Why's it okay to do this without discussing it?"

No air conditioning could cool or calm me down.

"Why is it okay that you can work from home?" he says. "It's my turn."

Sky-high fury fuels me.

If this were a true (T) or false (F) quiz, it would read:

1. In 1997, after Daughter #1 was born, I began working from home since it no longer made financial sense to pay childcare and commute to work.   T

2. The baby slept all morning while Son was at preschool.   T

3. I was antsy to do more than make food, clean house, do laundry.   T

4. The worldwide web had invaded the San Francisco market.   T

5. Content writers and copy editors were in high demand.   T

6. One day, my old friend called, raving about her job at BabyCenter, asking if I was interested in working from home as copy editor-editor-writer.   T

7. One freelance gig led to another.   T

8. I thrived, clocking 30 to 40 hours a week during naptime and nights.   T

9. Same story after Daughter #2 was born.   T

10. Four years later, after relocating to the   T
    other coast, I continued to work from home:
    writing, teaching yoga, teaching writing.

11. Mari worked long hours at the office in   T
    Marin then Manhattan.

12. Mari abhorred his commute.   T

13. Mari resented old-fashioned face time.   T

14. Mari reviled the dress code.   T

15. Mari left the office early every Friday to   T
    prepare for Shabbat.

16. Mari had to take time off for Jewish holidays.   T

"Not fair!" I shout. "You can't decide things like this on your own."

My head aches for the therapy sessions in New York to find our way back to each other, to redefine—☮ + ⌂, to stay together. My heart burns for the resentment I'd stockpiled over years and squandered in an instant. Am I too quick to anger, to judge? Too hell-bent on being me?

I bang upstairs to my office, putting an abrupt and unfinished end to our argument.

17. We could break our terrible   ?
    patterns.

"If we move there,"
New York, 2010

… I said to Mari,

redirecting the conversation to Israel, "then I no longer intend to abide by your version of Judaism or hide mine. I'll respect your decision not to use electricity or drive on Shabbat, but I don't have to do it that way, too."

How many decades had we been striking deals and speaking in conditional clauses?

He nodded.

"The kids have a right to know that Mommy believes X and אבא believes Y."

For years, Mari had begged me to present a united religious front. But we were more like a 1950s school district: segregated.

"Okay," he agreed.

"Okay."

(

... but?

were?

we?

Day in, day out

In early September, Mari and I celebrate our 26th wedding anniversary. I am not okay. Our conjugal strife is molasses-dense. All the emotional repair and healing we did happened too long ago, too far from here, in this house, where we are together: All. The. Time.

Day in, day out, I hear his hands pounding on his keyboard and his voice barking on the phone from his makeshift office down the hall. At lunch, when I glimpse the crooked kippa on his bald head, I flinch. I criticize what he wears, what he eats, what he says—an ugly behavior passed down from mother to daughter.

> since when is nagging genetic?

Unbeknownst to him, I scour *Poets & Writers'* classifieds for jobs in the Bay Area and plot my escape. After all, next year will be our seventh; we've never stayed longer than six in any one place.

With the electric shutters closed, darkness consumes us. Two tons of silence nestle in our bed. Minutes later, he snores like a tidal wave.

In the black, I rewind time. My eyelids flutter. I sleep. Think. Sleep. Think.

In a state of semi-consciousness, I envision myself living in a three-bedroom bungalow in Rockridge, working at a bookstore in Berkeley, alone, my kids scattered around the US.

Six Septembers ago, during draining tête-à-têtes, I pictured the five of us floating in different parts of the planet with no home base, understanding the only way to keep my family together was to move to the Middle East. Now, I'm no longer petrified.

In the morning, when I open my eyes, I remember it all.

Forearm Pose

A rude fly circles my space. September sun penetrates the open tent. Sweat cascades down the sides of my face. Yogeswari, our Swiss German instructor, introduces Pincha Mayarasana, telling us to place our forearms parallel to each other with two blocks between our palms and press palms into blocks before lifting our legs to Dolphin. The insect careens around me.

I watch Rachel. We met last year at Ella Yoga and instantly bonded over our conundrum: here for the husbands, men who put Israel before us. We struggle with the same stay-or-go—in the couple, in the country—issue on a regular basis. We grew up abroad, in public school, Hebrew School, Jewish summer camp, and youth group, but the men became super, duper Zionist.

During our three-hour drive to the Negev Desert together this morning, we griped about them and the ruthless heat. In between sentences, we cooed at Bedouin tents and abrupt cliffs, the stark and sandy, barren and vast landscape.

For years, I loathed this pose also known as Feathered Peacock. But over time, my relationship to some postures changed. Pincha and I made peace. When I lift my legs, I no longer banana my back but tilt my tailbone toward my heels while pushing my forearms toward the floor.

Inverting in this wall-less space intimidates me. I'm tough but terrified of falling. What is my greatest hurdle: fear, self-doubt, lack of trust? Whenever I confronted biology tests or boyfriend break-ups, my mother always asked what was the worst that could happen?

Chitta vritti nirodhah: if we control and curb our thoughts perhaps we won't be bound by the outside world.

I baby hop on the standing foot, one leg at a time, while Yogeswari says, "Perspective and prejudices are the biggest obstacle to our personal development. Rather than dwell on the negative, try to look at your circumstances and ask what you can learn from them."

I sigh, long and loud. Mari's reliance on laws and practices from past generations might not resonate with me, but yoga jargon does.

I am spiritual. This is my practice. Temples, god, rules, and traditions don't click as much as the belief in ourselves as creators and controllers of our own destinies. Surely I embraced this New Age rhetoric/movement/mood/lifestyle/system because I lost my own way of religion and, without realizing it, needed a substitute.

Outside, the sun swallows us. Inside, positive vibes thump like a nightclub. Yes, I can focus on the good. Yes, I love my husband. Yes, I want to stay together. And I play mental baseball, swinging the bat at all my buts—but my safety, but my parents, but my outsider-hood—to hit them far afield.

Yogeswari pumps her accordion, her upper arm muscles flexing with every in-and-out movement. "Come back," she says, "plant your feet."

Rachel and I land at the same time and say "wow."

Third Eye Chakra

Only two chakras left, but who's counting?

"To the wall," Rodney ordered us. We held the rope and hung butt up, head down, limbs bound like medieval prisoners. Blood and other bodily fluids gushed from my toes to my cheeks.

"We have to grow from this, right?" I joked, making everyone laugh, even Rod.

He yapped. "The poses are the tools, the instruments—not the goal. They're the tools to bring your mind and your body and your breath into harmonic convergence so that there's this sense of union."

Yes! I felt that union. When we stood upright, I closed my eyes for the room to right itself.

"Everyone away from the wall, big toes together and knees as wide as your hips. Begin to stretch your arms in front of you while folding forward into Extended Child's pose." He continued talking, using verbs like melt, shed, submit. "While you're here, ask yourself if you trust and act on your intuition."

Yes!

"This chakra," he said, "is associated with intuition. Working on it opens your mind to the bigger picture and different perspectives; it helps receive wisdom that can't be seen or heard by ordinary senses."

Even if my throat chakra was blocked, my third eye was open like a sliding glass door. After class, I told Rod about my burgeoning ambition to teach yoga.

"Go for it!"

Year 6: 2016-17

More signs

At Rosh Hashanah dinner, Mari proposes we share our greatest accomplishment over the past year. He says his start-up, while Son, visiting from San Francisco, says time-management skills, Daughter #1 army-related and top-secret, and #2, a marathon of exams. Last in a counterclockwise circle around the table, I hesitate; how much should I reveal to my children about my writing?

"You already know I'm writing a book about אבא and me," I say. Heads nod. "Well, I finished and now he needs to read it."

"Mazel tov," Son says.

"So," Daughter #2 chechems, "if you wrote about you guys and your story, that means we're in it too, right? Shouldn't we all read it?"

A Baptist choir chimes in with "yeah"s and "that's right"s!

I fiddle with my hands, clean the dirt under my nails.

This conversation, that question, my inability to answer, and the too-introspective-for-my-own-good mood for the past few months flash like signs to stow my book.

Signs, like superstitions[25], often have a negative connotation. While many consider them unfounded, illogical, irrational, I'm a believer.

Maybe I write in response to my slow comebacks: to answer after careful thought, to find the right words.

With ███, I never felt equipped to respond to their sharp, stinging remarks. With my kids, my fallback has often been "We'll see," hoping whoever has challenged me will dismiss it. But with age and wisdom, that line no longer works.

Instead, tonight, I say, "I hear you. I'm thinking. Can we eat?"

Un

■ calls: I warned you never to write about Mom and Dad's mess.

■ continues: I can't believe you published it!

■ spews: From now on, I consider myself an only child.

■ : Happy?

speakable

She says: You're kidding me, right?

She says: Because
I worked hard and am proud of it and wanted
to share it with the whole family, which includes you.

She says nothing. No response. Nada.

She didn't say: "Happy, no. Calm, yes."

But she wonders:
Had she sent her story to challenge their boundary?
To shake the status quo?
Or simply to take back her power?

She said-he said, California, 2006

"When your oldest child became a super Jew," my mother said.

"Oh, leave them out of it," my father grumbled.

"Okay, when your firstborn turned our lives upside down."

"Why are you always saying things like that?"

"Well, it's true, isn't it?"

Like a spectator sport, I sat, listened, watched as my parents volleyed back and forth in front of the therapist whom they recently started seeing at my insistence.

"Hold on, please," the Israeli American professional intervened. Minutes had passed: 75 down, 15 to go. Two back-to-back 45-minute appointments. "Your other child isn't in this room. Jennifer is. Look at Jennifer and talk to her."

I hadn't tallied how many times they tried—and failed—to address me. Their inability to speak directly confirmed something I'd always felt in my family of origin: overshadowed. Not less loved, but obliged to accommodate ██'s all-or-nothing ways, particularly when it came to our shared religion. I thought about the third chakra: the basic human right to see or to be seen. Mine tingled.

> was that my marital dynamic too?

At the end of the session, this man drew an unforgettable conclusion. "No one in any one family should have so much power. Your older child shouldn't hold this much power," he paused. "And you," he said, looking at my parents, "you gave it to them."

I felt affirmed, victorious, validated. As if this man gave me words I hadn't possessed and my parents an opinion they could no longer ignore.

The room was charged, electrons scurrying in every direction.

Sober

During Friday night dinner in our sparsely decorated sukkah, we don sweatshirts and jeans. Still, for October, it's unseasonably balmy and nothing like New York.

"Girls, what are your future plans?" my yoga student asks in her measured London accent.

During private lessons, we talk about books and travels, kids and countries. This week, I invited her and her husband for the holiday.

Daughter #1 always answers first. "I'm finishing the army next November and plan to study abroad. My older brother and grandparents and cousins are in San Francisco so maybe there."

"And why not study here?"

"Well, we moved here when I was 14. In the beginning, I was angry and didn't want to come, but it grew on me. I went to a good high school and am in an amazing Air Force unit. But the country's small. I want to live here later in life but need a break."

Our non-observant neighbor barbecues. The odors of grilled meat waft and mix well with our chicken couscous made hours ago and reheated in the oven.

"That's fair. I can see that," my student says. "And you?" she eyes Daughter #2.

Six weeks ago, Daughter #2 received her official envelope from the army summoning her for the First Call but only opened it this week at our insistence.

"I'm either doing army or national service," she says. "Either way, when I finish, I'm also going to study abroad."

Daughter #2 had recently expressed interest in taking a tour of U.C. Berkeley, her grandparents' alma mater, on our next trip to northern California.

"Oh. My." Our guests say in unison. "And you, parents, what would it be like to live here without your kids?"

My student and I have shared many intimate conversations. While I work her hamstrings in runners' stretch, she chatters to take her mind off the intensity.

"Me?" I ask, looking at Mari. He needs a new kippa.

even better: no kippa

He leans back against the sun-damaged pillow in the cast iron chair. Mooshy the street cat scrambles up our fence.

"If all three leave, I can't imagine staying."

My student nods slowly. My daughters clear the table. My husband heads for the house.

Something's wrong—and I think it's me. But is it emotional, physical, or physiological? Nature or nurture?

Still seated and abandoned by my family, I think now what?

Visceral

Mid-morning, my cell phone blinks and bleeps as if possessed by an extraterrestrial.

> ⚠ **Emergency alert: Extreme!**
>
> התרעת חירום: קיצונית!

When that shrill yowl starts, I dash down one set of stairs. Plie spine over legs. Squeeze eyes. Fist hands. Clench shoulders. Shake. Were Picasso to paint me, he could have called it *Woman Unraveling*. I screech the F word to my vacant house along with every other curse word in my vocabulary.

The furor stops.

Drill over.

Until next time.

Paschimottanasana Pose

At the end of Shelley's 90-minute Vinyasa class, I am cherry-faced and sweaty. As I fold over my legs, intense sensation surges like a giant sea swell. Impossible-to-prevent tears tumble.

Four letters zigzag through my thoughts: PTSD.

Do I suffer from an undiagnosed form of Post-Traumatic Stress Disorder?

Do I cry often and easily because I feel unsafe?

Have I failed to internalize the message with which my parents raised us to live fearlessly?

It's not a constant; the violence ebbs and flows. But during Operation Protective Edge, that haunting jangle stripped me bare.

When Shelley tells us to release, I sit up and close my eyes to still my trembling body.

Exemption

As soon as Daughter #2 opens the front door, I dash downstairs. Today were the initial exams for the IDF, a rite of passage for high school juniors. The start of the months-long army evaluation process, requiring them to miss school tests, projects, trips. Teachers comprehend.

Everyone travels to Tel Hashomer recruitment base for the day, but not everyone serves. Exemptions are reserved for expatriates, medical or psychological issues, moral objections, religious objections, married, pregnant, or parents, full-time Yeshiva students, religious Israeli Druze citizens, Arab Israeli citizens, and criminal records. ■ served soon after immigrating, before becoming Ultra-Orthodox, but none of their children do.

"Did you get it?" I ask.

"Some army doctor looked at my file and asked if I could shoot a gun. How am I supposed to know? He checked the medical exemption and told me they'll contact me to appear before a committee." She grins and pumps her fist.

Back in California, Daughter #2 arrived with a sharp cry and extra digits. Cosmetic, the pediatrician had concluded. She was 12 when we uprooted her, but the IDF doesn't care where you're born or how long you've been here if you can load and shoot, a requirement to pass basic training.

I rearrange our word problem: *If* I agreed to come to Israel for one decade—from first child entering army to last child exiting army—and *if* the last child is exempt from serving in the army, does that mean I, along with the last child, are free to leave?

   a. Yes, for obvious reasons

   b. No, it's more complicated than that

   c. Depends on other factors and family members

Extended Side Angle Pose

One humdrum Saturday morning, Daughter #2 asleep and Mari at synagogue, Daughter #1 and I go downstairs for a stretch-and-kvetch session. I lead. She talks incessantly, in need of a check-in, chitchat, chillax after concentrated 12-hour days at the base. I listen, relieved to hear how full her days are, how close her unit is, how much she's learning. When the subject of relationships arises, she drops words like international, interfaith, intermarriage.

"I'm not sure you got the memo. It's important to marry within the tribe. Celebrating holidays and parenting with someone from another faith is difficult. Even if it seems like I'm contradicting myself, is my message clear?"

She yeah, yeahs me. "But, if I fall in love with someone not Jewish and we have a ton of other things in common, then it's the way it might be." Droplets of perspiration coagulate on her temples. "It's more important to love someone no matter what religion. You taught us that."

Guilty—as charged. Proud—as can be.

"Yes, but, look at us, אבא and me. We're both Jewish, but we have such different views on how to create a Jewish household."

She yeah, yeahs me again. "You guys still love each other. Look at how well you raised us, how solid we're turning out, how connected we are to Israel and Judaism—even if we don't practice it the way we were brought up. You guys worked through those differences and made it work. Get it?"

Older and supposedly wiser, I am still slow with comebacks, at a disconcerting loss for words.

Shift

Early spring, my Californian cousin visits. During a casual Israeli meal of homemade hummus, diced cucumber-tomato salad, and creamy tehina, she cannot take her eyes off my soldier in her sandstone-colored uniform.

"Are you happy here?" she asks.

Daughter #1 puts down her pita. Daughter #2 continues eating. A visible fly on the wall, I listen.

"I didn't want to leave New York and all my friends, but when I look at our lives now, I think my experiences are much more profound. Israeli teens face reality and learn about the world in a way that my peers in the States don't. It was really hard, but yeah, I'm happy my parents came back, happy to be here."

My cousin and I catch eyes. I chew on my daughter's closing statement, full of admiration.

After

... the sun has set

... Mari and his father have returned from synagogue

... the table has been adorned with the ceremonial objects

... Mari deems everything in order

we take our seats around the table.

In fits and starts, in French and Hebrew, he leads the ritual feast marking the beginning of Pessach, chanting prayers, asking each of us—his parents and our girls—to participate.

"Tu veux lire?" he points to his childhood Haggadah[26].

I decline. No desire to read, to partake in the Seder, to be here.

If my mother were to see me now, age 51, she'd accuse me of sulking like a spoiled little girl.

It's late; we only start retelling the story of the liberation of the Israelites from slavery in ancient Egypt after nightfall. My stomach screeches.

Ultimately, they've acknowledged/held/tasted/smelled/chanted/asked/answered/shared/sang/read the story from start to almost finish.

"Voilà," Mari says, playing the happy host. "Time to eat."

He claps his hands, rubs his belly. Like a robot, I stand and steel myself to assume any-of-my-too-many-roles: Good Jewish Wife, Good Jewish Mother, Good Jewish Daughter-in-Law, Good Jewish Hostess.

Sixty-some minutes later, when we reach the last page, Mari and his parents say, "Next year in Jerusalem!" like most Jews do.

> except me... next year I plan to get as far away as possible

Come (What) May

I move my sweaters and jeans to the back of the closet to give my sundresses and sandals prime real estate.

"What's wrong?" Mari asks.

Words of apology catch in my vocal cords.

Sometimes marriage is so hard.

Marriage in midlife is even harder.

Maturing

and seeing one's

own

shortcomings:

the worst.

Triangle, New York, 2010

Seated in our standard spots—

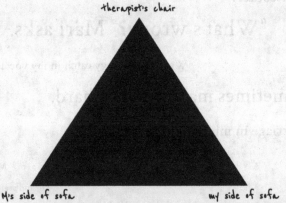

therapist's chair

M's side of sofa   my side of sofa

—my husband said, "I'm sorry I ever asked Jennifer to keep Shabbat and do things that made her so uncomfortable."

When, on the cusp of 24, he'd asked me to observe the Sabbath his way, I had no idea that yielding on something so significant would strip me of my identity as woman, wife, mother, Jew, individual.

"Thank you," I whispered.

Hormones

In the air-conditioned car, my friend Wendy rants about rude store clerks and road-enraged drivers.

"Now, enough about me. It's your go," she says with British authority.

"You want to hear the histrionics in my head?"

"You bet I do. It's been ages, and we need a proper catch-up. This will have to do before I pop off again. Go!"

A few years ago, when Wendy and I met at an English-speakers networking group, she said she'd been semi-grating, a term she coined about how she lives mostly here/Israel but often returns there/London to see her three sons and elderly mother. Ten years my senior, she's my match: secular, sententious, and judgmental.

As we enter my cul-de-sac, I unleash one long breathless story.

"Tell me something," she says. "Do you still get your period?"

I nod.

"In my humble opinion, I'd say you're perimenopausal. And I know these sentiments feel difficult, and

Jennifer Lang

you are frustrated here sometimes, but I also know you can't make some monumental, life-changing decision until those hormones have calmed down." She idles in front of my house. I pop out. "Right then, listen to me. Promise me you'll wait for your estrogen and progesterone to get to the other side. Yeah?"

"Yeah," I say and air-kiss her.

Roundtrip

On a steaming summer Friday, Mari, Daughter #1, and I cruise control to the Old City in Jerusalem for my 20-year-old Ultra-Orthodox nephew's baby's brit milah even though everyone advised us to reconsider.

For the past two weeks, Israeli Jews and Palestinians have clashed over metal detectors outside Haram esh-Sharif. Every one or two years, this holy site, claimed and contested by both Muslims and Jews, riles the army/police/Palestinian Authority/PM/people. The Jewish Quarter, our destination, is on alert.

We glide through the first half hour, with the remaining half up Route 1, where parked police vehicles block two lanes. We exit. Redirect to Route 443. Line up behind hordes of cars to pass security. Slow down. Crack our windows. Await border guards to perform terrorist profiling before waving us through. Pass barbed wire. Army bases. Mosques and minarets. WAZE guides us through Shu'afat, Wadi Al-Joz, Alsawana. See Hebrew University from a new vantage point: East Jerusalem. As in the sector of the city that was occupied by Jordan in 1948 and was excluded from the Israeli-held West Jerusalem at the end of the Arab-Israeli War. Since then, it's been occupied by Israel.

Today, streets are deserted, stores closed; all we hear is us, breathing.

"FYI, you guys," Daughter #1 says from the backseat, "I could get in so much trouble from my commander. We're not supposed to be here."

Mari shushes her. He clenches the wheel. I remind her she's not in uniform.

A few feet from the walls of the Old City, between the Temple Mount and Damascus Gate, a bunch of border police in protective vests line the street, preparing for protests.

"We're so late," I huff. "At this point, we'll probably miss the entire ceremony."

Uniformed men shout "I-ifshar" or impossible and "Ain c'nisa" as in no entrance.

We U-turn. When Mari asks what we should do, my fingers press HOME.

Redemption

Thirty-one days after the baby's birth, Daughter #2 and I step out of the car into the dry heat of Jerusalem. An oven on turbo grill. In her maxi skirt, she beseeches me to tie decorative ties near my neck to cover any trace of cleavage.

"Sorry, sweets," I say. "I'm 51, you're 18. This is who I am."

At the peak of the strive-to-blend-in phase, she forgets, between visits, that no matter what we do, how we dress, we stand out as different and less-than in ███'s universe. We missed the circumcision ceremony but made the baby's pidyon haben[27].

In the women's section of the windowless room, the marrieds wear elaborate scarves or wigs to cover every strand of hair, while the singles and littles are in long-sleeved ruffled and lacey dresses like Laura's on *Little House on the Prairie*. We are bare legged, but they sport thick stockings despite the desert's grip.

I search for any familiar female face who can vouch we belong, even if we look like interlopers.

"Hey, you came!" One niece screeches and runs to tell her little brother.

My nephew's one-month-old infant, adorned in gold jewelry and surrounded by tiny toile sacks of garlic cloves and sugar cubes, symbols of luck and health and other bubbemeises or grandmotherly fables, sucks on a pacifier, asleep in a bulky sterling silver soup tureen.

My nine-year-old nephew, the youngest of six and the only male family member allowed to cross the mechitza since he's under bar mitzvah age, greets us. I lean down to kiss his cheek. He retreats. In their house, our physical contact is allowed, but he's old enough to distinguish between public and private.

The women mill about their half of the room, kvelling over how cute, how quiet, how tall, how small the baby is. On the other half, a mass of males in black pants, white button-down shirts, black blazers, black kippas, and black top hats sing. Some have long payot[28] next to their ears; others tuck them behind out of sight. White tzitzit fringes hang over their pants. Every one of these outward, visible symbols of purity and devotion to HaShem[29] carries meaning. A man-boy whisks away the baby on the road toward redemption. The women peer through slats to watch. Like a Paramount movie set for *Yentl*. I stare at the men, swaying their bodies in joyful ecstasy, high on prayer.

When ▓ embraced this fervent form of Judaism three decades ago, I railed against them and their choices. But now I see the similarities between me standing on my hands in yoga or chanting OM with a room full of strangers and ▮ or spouse swaying and singing prayers. Aren't we all in search of the same thing: boundaries, guidelines, control? Don't we each long for community, acceptance, love?

Seeing my nieces and nephews who don't criticize me for not covering my hair or judge me for acting more goyish than Jewish, I know better now. My kids are their only close cousins, and I, their only aunt.

Scar

A week after my dermatologist removed an irregular-bordered, burnt brown spot on my shin, he called, saying: "Ze melanoma."

I froze. He tossed out distressing numbers: second biopsy, five-inch margin, to-be-determined stitches, one specialized eye test, three lymph node exams.

When Mari accompanies me for my follow-up appointment and asks about the plan, the doctor says, "Keep vigil" in stilted English. He leans forward in his chair. "Watch her back and every part of her body she can't see." Outside, the August sun menaces me like a bully. "That way you can alert her if anything's different."

Test results show the melanoma is superficial, on the skin, in situ. The scar heals. But the pinky mark serves as a permanent reminder of my mortality and of my mate, a man who will watch my back as long as I remain next to him.

Crown Chakra

"Ta da! You did it," Rod said like a cheerleader. One hundred and twenty minutes of yoga: the yoke or union of mind and body. "It's time to explore the crown chakra in our last pose."

Even I knew what came next: Savasana, whose Sanskrit name resounded more than its English translation. Corpse pose was my cue to exit before everyone laid down and closed their eyes. For years, he'd urged me to stay, explaining the importance of the final resting pose, but I pooh-poohed him, packed up, and disappeared. Today I was tired. Today I stayed. Today I listened.

Rodney rhapsodized about centering, about quieting the mind, about the seventh chakra. The more I breathed, the less thoughts nagged, the more my body surrendered.

"Four main things can block this chakra: shallow relationships, repressed emotions, ego, and fear of change."

His words wash over me. If nothing else, one aspect of my crown was far from blocked: fear of change. His narration grew fainter and fainter.

"Being on this mat is a huge step in healing your crown chakra. Remember you're here to reconnect with yourself, to listen to your soul's needs, to allow your intuition to lead you."

My entire body jerked from the bottoms of my feet to the top of my head.

Year 7: 2017-18

267

Missing piece

Shortly after the chagim, I treat myself to talk therapy. After summarizing my origin story, Israel roots, and roads not taken, I explain what brought me.

"Two women in my writing life sense I'm holding back, hiding behind my words. Either way, I'm intrigued."

The first was an MFA mentor and the second, a woman who led a writing retreat in Ireland and urged every memoirist "to work their shit out before coming to the page."

The skinny 60-ish-year-old woman in jeans and striped scarf takes notes. Born in Bulgaria, she immigrated to Israel as a girl and studied psychology in the US.

I remove my shoes and cross my legs on her home-office loveseat. I blabber nonstop until Son's return to San Francisco.

"Wait, let's stop there. What makes you teary?"

My lower lip shakes. I tell her it's easier to plow forward.

"Yes, but I want you to go inside for a moment. To address the sadness."

I close my eyes. "When he left, I realized what I did to my parents, when I moved to France and Israel. They never stopped me, always supported me. But now I'm the parent. I know how much it must have hurt. Our family will never be the same again. Like we're a puzzle with a permanent missing piece." I yank a Kleenex from the box. "My middle one is next."

When I look at the therapist again, she flashes a toothy smile. "Continue."

Meant to be

On a sunshiny November day, Mari and I drive to the Kiriya[30], where Daughter #1 meets us at the front gate. Soldiers of all ages clad in colorful uniforms and wool berets clipped on their shoulders walk with purpose. Today, her last, she's in jeans and a t-shirt.

"So," she says, opening her arms like a game show host, "welcome to where I spent almost every day of my life for the last two years."

I gawk at the high-end, modern, sleek building with its San Francisco Financial District feel. In the 15th story conference room, we deposit quiches and cakes for the separation celebration. At noon, her peers and superiors gather around the large rectangular table. Outside the window, cranes and construction sites monopolize the skyline.

"I'm so nervous," she says about the inevitable roasts and toasts and parting speech.

One by one, her officer, commander, lieutenant, and fellow non-commissioned officers—Scottish Israelis, South African Israelis, French Israelis, Sabras—praise her:

"You have a ruthless ability to delegate responsibility and to multitask, last minute, under pressure, well."

"I'm going to miss calling your office in the morning and hearing your chipper boker tov with that distinct American accent."

"I don't know how I'm going to survive without you."

I watch my daughter with awe, unable to believe this is the same girl who didn't want to come to this country. And, like my mother, who used to tell her friends that meeting Mari in Israel was bashert—Yiddish for fate—after enrolling me in a pilot French class in first grade, I think she was right. Maybe it was meant to be. Despite all the vicissitudes of our marriage and moves, Mari and I did the right thing.

Warrior II Pose

The typically Tel Avivian yoga studio's peeling paint and cracked walls exude shabby-chic appeal. An easy-going breeze waltzes through the arched windows. Cars beep outside; my flitting thoughts inside fade. A tattoo on the teacher's ribs emerges under her tank top. She asks if we've found our sweet spot, where our legs work without straining. My thighs burn.

Seven years ago, I wondered if I was warrior enough to live here. The thought still nags but not like before. Sometimes it's difficult, but mostly it's mundane: work, fill the fridge, prepare meals, pay bills. Israel might be locked in a never-ending feud over land, but American democracy is under threat. Not to mention that traveling abroad and witnessing history up close and personal still thrill me.

I never used to consider myself resilient, but even that has changed. In Sherri Mandell's *The Road to Resilience: From Chaos to Celebration,* she writes: "Resilience isn't being strong. Sometimes the first step is being weak. It's shattering when you need to, knowing there will be others to help pick you up." By her definition, resilience is my superpower.

The tattooed teacher tells us to feel the quiet strength of our body. Dusk descends. The guttural sound of a muezzin calls worshipers to prayer over the loud-speaker. Both mysterious and foreign. I wonder which of the ancient port city's three mosques is its source.

At the start, the Muslim recitation is one loud blur until it's not: La ilaha illa Allah.

There is no god except the One God.

While rooting my feet into the earth, firm and unwavering, I picture myself at my bat mitzvah, summer camp, youth group, reciting

שמע ישראל יהוה אלוהינו יהוה אחד

Hear, O Israel, the Lord is our God, the Lord is One
                                with conviction.

Truth

When my MFA-writer-friend Megan calls from California, I'm ready. After swapping manuscripts last month, we set today for feedback.

The first to read my revised memoir-in-vignettes, she starts: "While I think you've created a complex character who isn't always sure what she wants and who seems real and likable and flawed, I think this isn't about you and your husband and your inability to find home in the same geographic place as much as you and your personal journey to find it within yourself."

Tiny gasp. For the past year, I attributed the writing process—digging through old boxes, rereading old letters, flipping through old photo albums—as the culprit for the marital tension.

But the digging and rereading and flipping also showed me something else: barely 25, Mari and I were babies when we stood under the chuppah and said "I do." Since then, we've brought three exceptional beings into the world. Climbed mountain tops. Survived wars. Surgeries. Illnesses. Loss. Quarreled. Apologized. And one day, perhaps we'll walk down the aisle at our children's weddings, bike ride through Africa, and hold our grandchildren. None of this is trivial or easy. Staying together is perhaps harder than parting ways.

"There's something else. I was wondering if this woman who's married, a mom, healthy, homeowner, working, and a world traveler has a problem. Is it that she takes life for granted? Is she depressed? Or does she have a cup-half-empty attitude?"

Louder gasp. I'm committed to fixing my solar plexus chakra, to appreciating big-picture beauty.

"I hear you. Thank you for your honesty."

Megan's questions remind me of when, during the summer of our two-year wedding anniversary, everything from Israeli humidity to rude bus drivers to intrusive strangers made me cry; when I had no oomph to write my thesis, edit papers, or meet friends; when an American psychologist in Haifa diagnosed me with culture shock. Israeli culture no longer shocks as much as challenges me—to remain open-minded, to roll with the flow, to follow the signs.

After our call, I look at the marked-up manuscript against the revised one, head to my room, and study my face in the mirror, knowing the only antidote is an attitudinal overhaul.

Trade-offs

During a family reunion in New York City, my cousin sits next to me at dinner. Even though he's four years younger, he's always acted more like a big brother. ███'s in town too but doesn't join us unless we dine in select kosher restaurants.

"Hey cuz, how's life in Israel treating you?"

I tell him about Daughter #1's plan to study abroad, #2's army exemption and yen to study abroad, and my countdown.

"You're better off with Netanyahu than Trump. If I were you, I'd stay put."

Last year, in the days post-President Donald Trump's swearing-in, my Facebook feed exploded in rage. My writer and yoga communities declared he was not their president. My childhood and college friends attended marches from San Francisco to Los Angeles, from Des Moines to D.C.

The truth devastates me. Where I used to feel captivated by California's charm, I now feel flabbergasted by its failings: aggressive wildfires and school shootings and out-of-control homelessness. When I visit the Bay Area and see the mounting number of people on the streets, I worry for them and for the future of my homeland. America of today is unrecognizable compared to America of 2011.

With each move, I pined for the people and the place left behind. Romanticized the notion of home. But home is far from perfect, riddled with flaws. Every place, every relationship, every decision involves trade-offs, accepting the bad with the good, embracing the whole package.

My 80-year-old mother's ears prick up as she interrupts with "Did you hear what Trump did today?" before reading his latest Tweet aloud, using expletives that most grandmothers probably find unladylike.

And while everyone at the table rolls their eyes at her, I lean against my chair and contemplate my cousin's words.

Downward Facing Dog

Since the start of the New Year, since my return from New York, since my conversation with Megan, my studio has blossomed. Something's changed. I feel feathery, see distinctly.

Ten minutes into class, the door opens.

"Shalom, sorry, so sorry, traffic," the newcomer says. "I am Ayat." She points at her champagne-colored hijab, asking if there's a bathroom.

I multi-move: guide the group into Downward Facing Dog and show her the way. When she emerges, I'm dazed by looping, licorice-colored hair, Maybelline-proof eyelashes, silken blouse tucked into flowy pants. My regulars—American, British, South African, Brazilian, Turkish—dress in anything-goes, like t-shirts, tank tops, and leggings. They're not all Jewish. I'm accustomed to accents, to Other. Still, she stands out: the only Muslim.

When Ayat called to inquire about class, making sure it was women only, and told me she lives in Jaljulia, a neighboring Israeli-Arab town known for its hummus and car mechanics and massive new mosque, I didn't think she'd come. In miles, it's close; in culture, another planet.

Now, here, she scans the room, lifts her lower body, and breathes loudly. I see her legs shake.

When I expressed interest in teaching yoga as a language of peace for Arabs and Jews six years earlier, it seemed beyond my reach. But maybe, one day, it might materialize.

"Is this right?" Ayat asks.

I smile.

She whispers, "Hard, but beautiful."

A friendly titter fills the room. Her words cleave my heart. A reflection of where we live, who we are. Hard, but beautiful.

Unfathomable

My culture-friend Wendy and I peer over the balcony
for a bird's-eye view of the stage, watching a troupe of
older women cavort. I am mesmerized by the dancers'
lumpy legs and sagging breasts, by their grit and grace.

One woman with dyed black hair and broad, asym-
metric hips introduces herself, in Hebrew: "I'm 82.
After becoming widowed, I thought I'd never find joy
again. But now I have a boyfriend and dance."

As the performers zip into one-piece, seaweed green
parachute outfits, I think about Daughter #1's off-white
uniform. The music changes, a faster rhythm. The
dancers stay low as they glide and shuffle and chassé
across the floor. Without warning, the song stops.
A sinister, recognizable sound replaces it. A noise I
forever hoped never to hear again. In the stuffy room,
I quiver. A continuous ascending and descending tone.

Neither Wendy nor I say anything. No one does. I can't
decipher whether the air raid siren is inside or outside,
calculated or coincidental. Only when the women lie
on the floor in an artful heap—heads atop bellies, arms

across legs, feet pointed—like pick-up sticks does it register. It's intentional.

"Unreal."

"I know, right?" says Wendy.

In this teeny, tangled land, the personal and the political, the tranquil and the tumult, the creative and the destructive wrestle and wrangle every day. Just. Like. Us.

And in that state of mind, I feel present and awake, alive and aglow.

Freedom

While Jews around the globe sit at the Seder table, reading from the Haggadah, asking the age-old why-is-this-night-different-from-all-others question, I dine with a French friend in an Indonesian restaurant in Amsterdam where the answer zaps me.

This night is different because I'm free. Free from kosher-for-Pessach food. Free from Israel-imposed restrictions. Free from marital resentment.

Earlier this morning, we encountered an oversized vertical mural of Anne Frank's face in the industrial zone. Her iconic expression, straight white teeth, ebony black hair, gazed out, above, beyond. A quilt of colors crisscrossed her with four words in bold, cursive letters: Let me be myself. I quavered in my puffy coat.

It's taken me six years to separate from Mari's ways and shed the parental guilt I brought in my luggage. But it's taken 26 to unearth what was buried inside.

My friend and I marvel at the nasi goreng and gado-gado.

"I'm so glad I came," I say, relishing the fiery chili paste. "So happy to be here."

Free to be me.

In progress

After my MFA friend Alisa unpacks in our guest room, she tells me she studied architecture in college and must see the Bauhaus buildings in Tel Aviv. On Friday, I lead her through the crooked streets where most of the historic renovations are occurring. When my girls and I toured this neighborhood in 2011, we learned about the municipality's commitment to preserve the UNESCO heritage site. All these years later, I'm astonished by the transformation, feeling as if we're in it together.

Flash mob of stillness

Erev Yom HaZikaron, we fast-walk to the city center before sundown. Banks are locked. Stores are closed. Evergreens rustle. A pleasant April evening. Buses barricade Ahuzza Street near Yad Lebanim Memorial. We pass security checks. Say "Shalom." Open purses. Spot friends. Proffer kisses. Heave collective sighs. Close mouths. Mute cell phones. Await ceremony. Thousands gather to pay their respects, to remember seven decades: 23,646 fallen soldiers and 3,134 terror victims. Parents clasp children's hands. Grandparents admire uniformed recruits. Then, a one-minute, all-embracing siren. Cars stop. Our eyes shut. Nothing moves. Nobody breathes. Not even the trees.

Through her eyes

Since landing last week, our houseguest has asked nonstop questions: would I have uprooted if Mari hadn't insisted? Will I stay if the kids leave? Do I speak and read and understand Hebrew, or hide in an Anglo enclave? Given the situation, what's the best solution for Jews and for Palestinians? With Trump in America, Netanyahu in Israel, and terrorism everywhere, where's the safest place to live? Today, she asks the difference between the Memorial Day and air-raid sirens. I explain the former is constant while the latter fluctuates. Both hurt the ears. Both play with my psyche.

"I understand," Alisa says. "I know you don't love everything about this place, but do you feel how the shared history and communal loss binds you?"

Since her family's recent move from island to mainland, she's been searching for community. Tonight, while watching bereaved families place wreaths and share stories of their fallen soldiers, she beheld the most intense form of it in this country.

I sense it and smile.

"Okay, good. I wanted to make sure. Because if you didn't, I was going to have to think what to ask you next."

We lean towards each other and laugh.

Win-win

With all three kids out of the country, Mari and I stroll along Akko's Old City walls, remnants from once-upon-a-time rulers under the Byzantines, Crusaders, Ottomans, and others. A tawny teenager springs onto the ledge and scrutinizes sailboats docked in the port, container ships bound for Haifa, and the Mediterranean Sea taking a nap. He shouts in Arabic to a bobbing body below. Schoolchildren in matching caps stare, pointing at the boy in the water. We follow their fingers and squeeze hands. The ledge boy dives headfirst. The kids hoot. My stomach somersaults.

As we zig and zag under arches and through crooked passageways, street cats scurry and scrounge for scraps. Every corner we turn, we inhale their sour piss as they glare at us—the trespassers. We pass doorways and domes, castles and churches, synagogues and mosques with spellbinding, jaw-twisting names like Al-Jazzar, Al-Majadalah, El-Bahar, El-Zeituna. A tintinnabulation echoes through the alleys, perhaps Maronites or Franciscans, Latin Catholic or Greek Orthodox. A concert of sound, consonance of belief, harmony of customs. People—Jews, Muslims, Christians, Druze or Baha'is—breathe together. The Old City of Akko screams ancient, exotic, intriguing. It wakes me up like a foreign country even though it's only 90 minutes north.

"Did we ever come here?" I ask. "There's no way we missed this. You can practically see our old apartment."

We squint, searching south in the hills of Haifa, where we spent our young adult years.

That evening the port is alit like a scene from *Arabian Nights*. Speed boats and glossy yachts cruise the harbor. We board a boat playing brash Arabic music along with hijab-wearing Muslim women and religious Druze men with white skullcaps and women in monochromatic kaftans. A girl with obsidian eyes stares at us, the token Jews. I think about Ayat and what she might feel every time she enters my yoga studio.

The next day, we meander through the souk: butchers next to fish mongers next to produce vendors next to bakeries next to spice sellers and coffee grinders next to touristy tchotchke stands and jewelry stalls selling evil eye amulets and gold hamsah charms. In this corner of the world, symbols, superstitions, signs, and supernatural forces are embedded into the cultures and countries. They serve as a container, provide comfort.

When we enter Hummus Said, an unassuming restaurant with a 4.5-star TripAdvisor rating, a handful of sweaty men chop, dice, soak, stir, mash, grind, and fry at a frenetic pace. Diners clasp hot, puffy pita in lieu of silverware, half-circling their wrists in an artful swipe around the chickpea spread. A movement I have yet to master.

Ordinarily, I feel self-conscious, stamped Other whether in America, where I never hold back from speaking my mind like an Israeli, or in Israel, where I always say please and thank you like an American. But here, walled in with so many different people, I blend in and belong with everybody else.

Here, being Other doesn't mean either-or, all-or-nothing, bifurcated.

Here, in this country, I am mostly American, legally French, and sometimes Israeli.

It reminds me of a triad of contemplation on discernment and interconnectedness in yoga: I'm not you, I'm something like you, I'm nothing but you.

A win-win—if I drop the drama and move out of my way.

If I look through beginner's eyes.

If I point my vectors in the same direction.

If I exercise my personal right of return.

Savasana

Lying on my back, my shirt clinging to my overheated torso, I float. The Indian instructor blathers on and on, in English, about the sympathetic and parasympathetic nervous system, about the body's need to restore after a robust physical practice, about letting go. My heart chakra thumps. My root chakra tickles.

Thanks to our בית ריק, Mari and I checked into an Airbnb in Tel Aviv—also known as the Non-Stop City—for two nights. On this Shabbat morning, he's at synagogue, while I'm at Yoga Light studio.

On the wood floor, I feel good, sustained, safe. My monkey mind rollercoasters over realizations: how Mari and I have weathered almost a dozen major moves, how my crying coping mechanism has waned, and how he doesn't dither no matter what happens to me or my family of origin.

The teacher stops talking. I succumb, arms by my sides, legs turned out in Corpse pose. Dead and so alive.

I-can-stay thoughts flash like a disco club strobe. I can stay if Mari will live with me, and we can watch over each other's aging bodies. I can stay if I listen to my authentic self. Heed my throat chakra. I. Can. Stay. Like the Phillip Phillips' lyrics sung by the Jerusalem Youth Chorus, I can make this place my home. My mind stops seesawing.

A surprising stillness settles in my bones: chitta vritti nirodhah.

EPILOGUE: H☉E

Daughter #1 prepares to leave for college in New York. Daughter #2 extends her national service for a second year, deciding against studying abroad. Son moves from the west to the east coast. Mari works excessive hours to grow the business. I expand my writing class repertoire.

My decision to remain in Israel emboldens me.

"Je suis fier de toi," Mari says.

I'm proud of myself too.

"What's changed?" Friends—Judy, Marcia, Megan, Wendy, Shani, Alisa—ask.

"I bent back."

Foreign Language and Transliteration

Hebrew and Arabic are written in their own abjads, and Yiddish uses the Hebrew alphabet. Like with *Places We Left Behind: a memoir-in-miniature*, I used the Roman alphabet to transliterate certain words and expressions. When it comes to transliteration, there are many ways to spell some words.

Publication History

Excerpts from my memoir were previously published in different forms:

Crack: "Shazam" and "Back-up plans" and "Downward Facing Dog" in Ghost City Press micro-chap (2022)

Ducts: "As if" excerpted from "An Analphabetic Story of Consonants" (2017)

Consequence Forum: "Suspended Animation" (2021)

NPR Hanukkah Lights: "Split at the root" excerpted from "The View from Masada" (2018)

Ascent: "The F bomb," "Meaningless," and "Ceasefire" appeared in "Fifty Days of Summer 2014" (2017)

Hadassah Magazine: "ॐ" excerpted from "In Israel, Chanting 'Om' Between Missiles" (2023)

Bacopa Literary Review: "90 Seconds to Shelter" (2019)

The Forward: "Redemption" excerpted from "Visiting My Ultra-Orthodox Brother, a World Apart" (2017)

Flash Nonfiction Food: 91 Very Delicious, Very True, Very Short Stories: "Win-win" (2020)

Places We Left Behind: a memoir-in-miniature (2023) has won many prizes:

Finalist for Autobiography/Memoir, Foreword Reviews Book Awards 2023

Finalist for Women's Literature Non-Fiction, Next Generation Indie Book Awards 2024

Finalist for Adult Nonfiction, Wishing Shelf Book Awards 2023

Finalist in Multicultural Nonfiction, American Legacy Book Awards 2024

Finalist in Multicultural Nonfiction, American Book Fest's 20th Annual Best Book Awards 2023

Finalist in Multicultural Nonfiction, Independent Author Network Book of the Year Awards 2023

Pushcart Prize nomination for "Hand in hand," Vine Leaves Press 2023

Gold Book Award Winner, Literary Titan 2023

Finalist for book cover design, Wishing Shelf Book Awards 2023

Acknowledgments

While writing and birthing a book is a long, mean-dering journey that can feel lonely at times, it is all about community for me. I would never have walked or stayed on this path if not for certain people. A combi-nation of teachers, mentors, peers, friends, classmates, colleagues, students, and now, readers. Some taught me about the craft of writing, while others asked keen ques-tions, challenging me to think deeper or differently, to look through another lens, to begin anew. Some simply believed in me, urging me to believe in myself.

I would not be here, a published author of two books, without:

Mari and our gorgeous grown-up-ish children, who everything my actions and reactions.

My father, who transmitted all that he had gleaned from his Eastern European immigrant parents—Yiddishkeit, tzedakah, Israel—and my mother, who taught me the importance of sharing our differences.

My Vine Leaves Press clan, spearheaded by Jessica Bell and Amie McCracken, who supply unconditional support. The VLP publishers believe in good stories and diverse voices, which is especially meaningful given today's changing, charged climate.

Barbara Hurd, who planted the seed that maybe I should ask a different question, followed a couple of years later by Megan Vered, who insisted I reframe the question.

Lisa Romeo, Nancy Stohlman, and Chelsey Clammer, who edited various versions and emboldened me to see this story to the end.

Alice Lowe, Allison Hong Merrill, Amy Mindell, Anne McGrath, Kim Rogers, Magin LaSov Gregg, Mary Heitkamp, Nina Gaby, Nina Lichtenstein, Megan Vered, Sharon Epel, Stephanie Barton, and Tracy Lynch, who either read and responded to early, messy, overwritten iterations or read and responded to my frenzied attempts to find the heart of the story.

Kathy Fish's Fast Flash virtual community, who encouraged me to write about my little Israeli life in compressed prose.

My greater Raanana community who listened, nodded, and nurtured me while I navigated this journey.

My Sage yoga students, who expressed interest in my now obsolete blog, Open to Israel.

I thank each and every one of you from my first to my seventh chakra.

Readers' Guide

Did you read Jennifer Lang's first book, *Places We Left Behind: a memoir-in-miniature,* which ended in 2011? If so, did it enhance your reading of *Landed*? If not, did it make a difference?

Why do you think yoga was so important to the narrator?

Was Jennifer too open with her children? Too honest about the marital issues?

In "Truth," when her writing friend Megan asks, "I was wondering if this woman who's married, a mom, healthy, homeowner, working, world traveler has a problem. Is it that she takes life for granted? Is she depressed? Or does she have a cup-half-empty attitude?" Do you see that as a pivotal moment for the narrator? Do you have a friend who has given you honest constructive feedback that changed you or your perspective?

History—what happens in the country where she lives as well as in the country where she's from—plays a significant role in the narrator's life. Take "Headlines" as one example. Is it the same for you? Are you as affected by world events? In what way?

Like in her previous book, *Places We Left Behind,* Lang does many unconventional things on the page: redaction, symbols, lists. Are they effective? If so, why? Or do you find them jarring? Why?

The narrator swears—in anger, frustration, danger. Does it bother you when you read curse words?

What word would you use to describe their marriage? For those of you who are in long marriages, what word encapsulates yours?

Why do you think it took Jennifer another six years to finally find home? What took so long?

Does this story feel more personal or universal? What and why?

Are you superstitious? Do you believe in signs? Symbols? Can someone be superstitious and believe in a higher being or do you think they're mutually exclusive?

Did you learn anything new about Israel or Judaism? If so, what?

Endnotes for curious readers

1 It appears over 700 times throughout both the Old and New Testaments; it's the center point which unifies all of nature, as with Shabbat.

2 A set of dietary laws dealing with the foods that Jewish people are permitted to eat and how those foods must be prepared according to Jewish law or halacha.

3 The Jewish religious concept of domestic harmony and good relations between spouses.

4 Originally a Persian word, balchan morphed into balagan as it migrated from Turkey to Russia to Lithuania to Palestine during the late 19th century.

5 A makeshift mechitza to separate men and women; according to halacha, a partition dividing men and women is derived from the Babylonian Talmud to preserve modesty and attention.

6 Elohim is the more common name for God in the Old Testament, while Adonai is used in worship.

7 A type of cooperative agricultural community of individual farms pioneered by the Labor Zionists between 1904 and 1914.

8 A Hindu author, mystic, and philosopher between the 2nd century BCE and the 4th century CE, Patanjali is believed to have written the *Yoga Sutras*, a classical yoga text.

9 Developed in 1997, Anusara yoga combines spirituality with a system of biomechanical principles derived from Iyengar yoga; main concepts include flowing with grace, aligning with nature, and following your heart.

10 A combination of sho, meaning beginner or initial, and shin, meaning mind.

11 Yiddish for grandfather; Baba is grandmother.

12 Humility (n.): early 14c., "quality of being humble," from Old French humelite "humility, modesty, sweetness" (Modern French humilité), from Latin humilitatem (nominative humilitas) "lowness, small stature; insignificance; baseness, littleness of mind," in Church Latin "meekness," from humilis "lowly, humble," literally "on the ground," from humus "earth," from PIE root *dhghem- "earth." And, what I wonder, is the connection between humus/earth and hummus/a Middle Eastern paste made of chickpeas mashed with oil, garlic, lemon juice, and tehina?

13 A very liberal branch of Judaism, it considers Jewish law as non-binding and the individual Jew as autonomous and is characterized by little stress on ritual and personal observance, and by a great openness to external influences and progressive values.

14 A set of small black leather boxes with leather straps containing scrolls of parchment inscribed with verses from the Torah, tefillin are worn by adult Jews during weekday and Sunday morning prayers.

15 Fou (adj., masc.): mad, insane, nuts, bonkers, demented, lunatic, nutty, kooky, deranged, aberrant, off his rocker, cuckoo, unhinged, unstable, unbalanced, unsound.

16 Jews born in Israel are named for the thorny cactus, otherwise known as prickly pear, for its thick skin and sweet, soft insides.

17 Recitations of prayers, mantras, and chants are counted on mala prayer beads customarily used in both Buddhism and Hinduism; Buddhist malas traditionally have 108 beads, said to signify the 108 human passions that Avalokiteshvara assumed when 'telling the beads'; there are said to be a total of 108 energy lines converging to and from Anahata, the heart chakra; there are 54 letters in the Sanskrit alphabet, each has masculine and feminine, shiva and shakti, 54 times 2 is 108.

18 No driving, no spending money, no watching TV, no talking on phone, no turning on computer, no listening to music, no cooking, no, no, no, no, no, no, no, no, no.

19 Israelis who cannot return to their families for religious, financial, or emotional reasons, as well as Jews from around the world who have left their families to enlist.

20 Founded by 70 families who were residents of the former Israeli settlement of Netiv HaAsara, which was evacuated because of the Camp David Accords; the original moshav was named for ten soldiers who were killed in a helicopter accident south of Rafah in 1971.

21 One of the five niyamas—the moral codes or social contracts—outlined in Patanjali's *Yoga Sutras*.

22 Israeli self-defense system.

23 en.wikipedia.org/wiki/Route_443_(Israel-Palestine).

24 First constructed in 1882, Celica was formerly a military barracks for the Austro-Hungarian army, then a prison for over a century, and eventually a hostel, each of its 20 cells designed by a different artist to create a unique atmosphere.

25 Superstitions trace back to early 13th century, to superstitionem, Latin for excessive fear of the gods, religious belief based on fear or ignorance and considered incompatible with truth or reason or more literally, "a standing over" from superstare.

26 A Jewish text that sets forth the order of the Passover Seder; for every Jew to tell their children the story from the Book of Exodus about God bringing the Israelites out of slavery in Egypt

Kadesh—reciting kiddush

U'Rechatz—washing the hands

Karpas—eating a vegetable dipped in salt-water

Yachatz—breaking the middle matzah

Maggid—reciting the Haggadah

Rachtzah—washing the hands a second time

Motzi—reciting the blessing HaMotzi

Matzah—reciting the blessing and eating the matzah

Maror—eating the bitter herbs

Korech—eating a sandwich of matzah and bitter herbs

Shulchan Orech—eating the festive meal

Tzafun—eating the afikomen

Beirach—reciting grace

Hallel Nirtzah—reciting Hallel, psalms of praise; the promise that God will accept our service

27 There are two ceremonies to celebrate the firstborn boys' arrivals: the brit milah followed by the pidyon haben, a mitzvah whereby a Jewish son is redeemed by use of silver coins, perhaps being redeemed from their firstborn status, which was stigmatized after the Ten Plagues, or their obligation to serve as a priest, or from human sacrifice. It's relatively rare; a family does not perform the ceremony if its firstborn is either a girl, born by caesarian section, preceded by a miscarriage, or if either grandfather is a Kohen or a Levite.

28 Sidelocks or sideburns worn by some men and boys in the Orthodox Jewish community based on an interpretation

of the Tanakh's injunction against shaving the sides of one's head; literally means corner, side, edge.

29 HaShem or the Name is employed to refer to God when not in prayer.

30 In central Tel Aviv and one of the first IDF bases since the country's founding in 1948, mainly command, administrative, communications, and support functions.

Vine Leaves Press

Enjoyed this book?
Go to *vineleavespress.com* to find more.
Subscribe to our newsletter:

9 783988 320872